Evan Frederic Morgan
Viscount Tredegar

The Final Affairs, Carnal and Financial

Including how Evan's Executors wound up his Estate

Hon. Evan Frederic Morgan
2nd Viscount Tredegar

ISBN 10 1-905914-24-5
ISBN 13 978-1-905914-24-1
Published by William P. Cross
Book Midden Publishing
58 Sutton Road
Newport
Gwent
NP19 7JF   United Kingdom

Evan and Chums

"Reader! Here is the curtain rung up on each passing mood, on each fleeting fancy, and every scene is set wrought from the play of Life. The Heart stands prompter. The Pen and Paper actors. Here is Love, Joy, Sorrow, Reflection, a cosmopolitan piece, ill-shapen, since."

EVAN MORGAN: FRAGMENTS: 1916

Evan Frederic Morgan : The Last Viscount Tredegar
Brief Time Line

1893 : 13 July- Evan Frederic Morgan born Chelsea, London. Father - Courtenay Charles Evan Morgan; Mother - Lady Katharine Agnes Blanche Carnegie. A first child. Courtenay and Katharine married at Kinnaird Castle, Brechin, Scotland in 1890. Evan's sister Gwyneth Ericka Morgan born two years later in 1895.

1890s : Evan and Gwyneth grow up in London and visit Ruperra Castle, South Wales and Kinnaird Castle, Brechin.

1901 : Evan is a Royal Page at the Coronation of King Edward VII. Meets Peter Churchill.

1905 : Evan attends a preparatory school in Brighton. Failed attempt to kidnap Evan.

1907-10 : At Eton with James Lonsdale Bryans and George Rodney. Leaves Eton "under a cloud". Travels with Katharine abroad.

1913 : Evan exhibits paintings at the Paris Salon. Evan's father becomes 3rd Lord Tredegar.

1914 : Evan is 21. Goes to Christ Church College, Oxford. Gwyneth is presented at Court.

1914 - onwards : Evan is part of the wave of new poets, artists etc at Café Royal and later the Eiffel Tower Restaurant , London. He is also a regular at the Randolph Hotel, Oxford. Meets Cyril Hughes Hartmann, an editor of 'Oxford Poetry'. Even is sent down from Oxford.

1915 : Evan joins the Welsh Guards. Photographs (in uniform) taken with his father.

1916 : Publishes 'Fragments' - first book of poems. 1916 : Visits Garsington Manor, Oxford and signs the Visitors book on 16 July 1916. Befriends Aldous Huxley.

1917 : Goes to work as an unpaid Hon. Secretary in Whitehall. Regularly ill and receiving intensive treatment for lung disease.

1917 : Publishes 'Gold and Ochre' second book of poems.

1918 : Evan spends time in Algiers, North Africa – because of his health.

1918-9 : Evan resigns his commission but is seconded by Sir George Riddell to work with the British Press Corps at Versailles during the Paris Peace Conference. Evan becomes a Roman Catholic. Evan revels in the seedier fringes of Parisian night life.

1920-1 : Publishes 'Psyche' - an unfinished fragment, and a novel called 'Trial by Ordeal'.

1920 : Evan goes to USA. Rumours that he is to become a monk and renounce birthright.

1920-1 : Evan appears in fiction as 'Ivor Lombard' in Aldous Huxley's 'Crome Yellow'. A dedication to Evan in Ronald Firbank's novel 'The Princess Zoubaroff' causes trouble.

1920s : Evan spends time in Paris and Rome with Nina Hamnett and is introduced by her to Aleister Crowley. Travels extensively through France, Italy, the Mediterranean and North Africa. In Spain with Cyril Hughes Hartmann.

1923 : Evan is lampooned by Ronald Firbank as 'Hon. Eddy Monteith' of Intriger Hall in 'The Flower Beneath the Foot.'

1923-4 : Evan a regular at Cavendish Hotel. Publishes 'At Dawn, Poems Profane and Religious.' Evan is presented to King George V and Queen Mary as a Chamberlain to Pope Pius XI , during Royal visit to the Vatican. Evan enrols at Beda College, Rome.

1924-5 : Gwyneth disappears- after 5 months a body is fished out of the River Thames. Evan fails to attend the funeral, as in Rome. Gwyneth buried in Putney Vale Cemetery. Evan ejected from Beda leaves Rome June 1925 goes to Oxford. Writes ' In Pace' to exorcise ghost of Gwyneth.

1925-6 : Evan becomes the Conservative Parliamentary candidate for Limehouse. Courtenay made a Viscount and late becomes an ADC to King George V.

1927-8 : Publishes ' The Eel and other poems'. Dec 1927 : Engagement to Hon. Lois Sturt who becomes a Roman Catholic marries Evan at

Brompton Oratory on 21 April, 1928. Huge amounts of money set aside for a matrimonial home. Evan goes to Germany.

1929 : 'City of Canals' published. Evan elected to Royal Society of Literature. Travels to Canada attracts criticism for comments on the state of Canadian culture and country's infrastructure.

1929-33 : General Election: Evan loses to Clements Attlee at Limehouse. Later Evan becomes prospective Parliamentary candidate for Cardiff Central. Withdraws for National Labour Candidate. Lois moves to 'Mumpumps' and sues Evan for divorce, action later lapses.

1934 : Death of Courtenay Morgan, Evan becomes 4th Lord Tredegar, 2nd Viscount and takes his seat in the House of Lords. Evan has Gwyneth exhumed and buried at St Basil's, Bassaleg, near Newport.

1937 : Lois Sturt dies in Budapest, aged 37. Hey day of Tredegar House parties and long haul world travel.

1939: Evan marries Princess Olga Dolgorouky in Singapore. Honeymoon in Bali.

1940 : Evan in the Monmouthshire Home Guard. Olga makes a good impression in Newport as Lady Tredegar.

1942-3 : Evan is attached to Royal Corps Signals (MI 14). Court Martialled and retires from the Army.

1943 : Crowley visits Tredegar House. Bust of Evan completed by Prince Bira of Siam for 50th birthday. Evan's marriage to Olga annulled.

1945: Evan shuts Tredegar House, finances decline. Looks to marriage to secure a better financial future and pay off tax debts.

1947-9 : Rejects handing over some of the Tredegar Estate to John Morgan. Falls ill in Rome, returns to UK and goes into the Middlesex Hospital, London. Evan is sent home to die.

1949 : 27 April. Evan dies at Honeywood House, Rowhook, Dorking, aged 55. Buried Buckfast Abbey, Devon. Representative of Evan's Executors meets the Solicitor of Inland Revenue.

Introduction

The Name of Morgan and Ancient Links

A Livery Button: Morgans of Tredegar House[1]

"Born of the sea- or son of the sea", is the literal meaning of the surname Morgan. The name is of Cymric origin from the words 'muir', sea and 'gin', begotten. Translated into Greek the name becomes Pelagius," 'of the sea'. Legends and classic lore, interwoven with the name of Morgan, have to do with King Arthur, who was carried away to the Isle of Avalon by his sister in the Fata (fairy) Morgana called in the old Arthurian romances which Tennyson's 'Idylls of the King' have made familiar to us all, Morgan le Fay."... [2]

Co-incidentally Lord Alfred Tennyson composed a part of this epic verse near the Morgan family homeland in Caerleon (a village only a few miles from Newport, South Wales, occupied for a long time by the Romans [3] and famed as a possible site of Camelot). One scribe expounds:

"It was to Caerleon that Tennyson turned when he was writing 'Idylls of the King' in 1856. He lodged in the Hanbury Arms [a Public House], where he could look out over the River Usk, and went on long walks through the surrounding countryside to draw inspiration.

[Today] Visitors can still sit in 'Tennyson's Window' - here it doesn't take much imagination (or liquid refreshment) to wander back through time ..." [4]

Gla-Morganshire

Glamorganshire in Wales, which derives its name from Morgan, was the kingdom of King Morgan, who lived in the eighth century, and was the founder of the family of Morgan. He headed a line of Welsh Kings and Princes, all famous warriors. It is said that Morgan of Gla-morgan established the form of trial by jury and not Alfred the Great of England as is generally supposed. [5]

Another text makes this reference to the Morgan roots:

"The family of Morgan," we quote Archdeacon Coxe, "being so conspicuous in the history of Wales, the Welsh bards have exerted their utmost ingenuity to trace its origin and lineage. Fanciful genealogists derive it from the third son of Noah, and modestly affect to correct the mistake of the English, in carrying the pedigree to Ham, his second son. Some stop with Brutus, the conqueror of Britain; others with Beli, one of the British kings; and some are even content with Caradoc, or Caractacus. It is, however, generally agreed that Cadwir the great, Lord of Dyfed, who died in 1084, was their great ancestor." [6]

Evan Morgan

Hon. Evan Frederic Morgan (1893-1949)(4th Baron Tredegar, the last Viscount Tredegar, of Tredegar House, Newport, Monmouthshire, South Wales and Honeywood House, Rowhook, near Dorking in Surrey) was a poet, dandy and aristocrat, who "lived riotously..entertaining extravagantly and pursuing a love life among a wide range of members of his own sex". [7] Evan relished telling everyone he was descended from Welsh Kings and Princes of Wales. In an equally long repeated alternative history he revelled in telling that his family had a not inconsiderable link with the celebrated Black Knights who appear in Welsh mythology and Arthurian legend, and who were succeeded by the famed Knights Templar.

One text on this subject of the Black Knights [8] captures the claim and declares Evan's antecedent links, also sweeping in King Arthur, " Evan Morgan, Viscount Tredegar, was a well known eccentric in the 1930s.. and mysteriously dubbed by the occultist Aleister Crowley[9] " the most fitting to wield Excalibur....." [10] An explanation is given to this as follows...." The latter [i.e. the claim about Excalibur] perhaps being due to the Morgan families' ancient descent from the Llewellyn's, who claimed Arthurian ancestry, as part of their tradition of Bardic patronage.... This family also intermarried with the Pembroke de Clares at an early date, bringing them into the orbit of [the] Black Knights. So the Morgans too fall into this lineage, perhaps one of the last in a long line of such families." [11]

Evan Frederic Morgan, Viscount Tredegar: The Final Affairs, Carnal and Financial

This book is the first part of a two-part outline or "fragments" (co-incidentally the title of Evan's first book of poems, from 1916). But what follows are fragments of a different kind, more an assortment of narratives from the life and times of Evan Morgan providing a few new anecdotes as well as a backward glance at material that is not sufficiently covered in the earlier books 'A Beautiful Nuisance', 'Aspects of Evan' or 'Not Behind Lace Curtains.'
12

The sub-title of this current volume is "Final Affairs, Carnal and Financial". In using the word 'Carnal' it is to offer some insight into the worldly, earthly and temporal side to Evan as well as facts about his relationships, homosexuality and inner passions. The book also contains a summary of Evan's final financial affairs, drawn from his Executors' dealings with the Inland Revenue from 1949 onwards.[13]

It is hoped the eclectic mix covered will be of interest to readers. The second volume with a sub-title "[Evan's] Final Affairs, The Aftermath" will also combine other tales about Evan, with a summary of the disposal of his last two homes, the Morgan family seats of Honeywood House, near Dorking, in Surrey and Tredegar House, Newport, South Wales.

La folie de la grandeur
Evan's Delusions of Grandeur

To the end of his life Evan Morgan wanted to impress his Society acquaintances with passing references such as telephoning to the Pope most evenings"[14]. Yet as his financial standing became more and more insecure on account of his worsening income tax arrears, coupled with a serious health condition he became a prisoner as trapped and confused as a wild beast in a zoo.

Evan knew he was shortly to die; he was a man who had seen life at many angles, usually the odds were in his favour, but now the daggers were moving dangerously towards his heart.

In such an acute state of suffering his *'La folie de la grandeur'*[15] (delusions of grandeur) once a central characteristic during Evan's existence fell completely flat, as no one was listening to him anymore. One diarist records:

"He [Evan] has an enormous number of acquaintances – I fear no friends." [16]

By 1945 Evan was particularly isolated as he was *persona non grata* within Royal and Court circles; it was common knowledge that over the decades his high ranking, well placed, regally connected cousins[17] had saved Evan from exposure over his illegal life style.

But as Evan celebrated the end of the war the latest turn of events was a last straw for one monarch. This followed Evan's run-in with Queen Mary over an exhibition of lewd photographs taken at a party showing naked men rollicking together and indulging in homosexual activity. To make matters worse some of the participants in action in the pictures were members of Queen Mary's own family, allegedly this included nude snaps of her dead son, the tragic Prince George, Duke of Kent.[18] She had seen the exhibition by chance on visiting Evan's London flat. [19] Queen Mary had a reputation for gate-crashing, with no mention of her plans in advance in the Court Circular.

According to Evan's intimate chum, Robin Bryans [20] the Queen "marched out of the house with more dangerous intention. Evan's panic [about the photographs and the Queen's wrath] lasted until the day he died." [21] "Queen Mary's favourite Bohemian" [22] was catapulted down to earth. Evan died on 27th April 1949 from cancer,[23] aged 55 without being reconciled with the rulers of the House of Windsor.

Whilst Clement Attlee,[24] "the Prime Minister was represented at a requiem Mass for Evan, Viscount Tredegar",[25] the British Royal family did not send a representative to *any* of Evan's memorial services, albeit the Carnegie cousins (Evan's mother's well-connected family) were in attendance in their own right.

The Carnegies also purged Evan's life secrets from reaching public knowledge by the disposal of a black box of personal papers at Honeywood House which he had deemed be placed in the hands of "the elegant" [26] Henry Maxwell,[27] who was described by one observer as " the greatest love ...of [Evan's] life"[28] and the bookish Cyril Hughes Hartmann [29], from whom Evan craved constant admiration as a fellow poet.

In his will, Evan chose these two long standing followers in order that they could write his biography. The (almost certain) destruction of the black box (with its contents) extinguished this key component of Evan's last wishes ever being fulfilled. In 1949 British laws (passed in the 19th Century[30]) criminalized homosexuality and offenders had no mitigation, if apprehended. The truth about Evan's life was only rolled out decades later in dribs and drabs. Many mysteries still remain. Robin Bryans claims he salvaged some personal items belonging to Evan, alleging that "while Robin Chester [a solicitor friend of Evan going back to their Eton days] [and others] busied themselves with settling claims against Evan's estates in a number of countries, I [Bryans]shuttled between Evan's various homes to recover letters and religious impedimenta which the philistine John Morgan [Evan's cousin and penultimate heir] might destroy." [31] Nevertheless Evan's Executors acted quickly and ruthlessly, besides which the legal firm of *Tozers of Teignmouth* (concerned with the interests of Buckfast Abbey, where Evan had been buried) assumed draconian control of the Morgan family seats and the contents of Evan's last homes.

Evan's Oedipus Complex: Mother Love

A mention is justified in Evan's final affairs of Lady Katharine Agnes Blanche Carnegie, [32] his much maligned mother. As Evan's terminal illness brought his flamboyant life of travel and adventure to a sad and bitter anti-climax he had to live more and more at Honeywood House where by the mid-1940s his mother had retreated from the world at large.

Short trips to Italy and the West coast of Ireland gave Evan some respite and prayer. In the end Evan returned (in remorse) to his Catholic faith and arranged that his beloved brethren, *viz* the monks of Buckfast Abbey, Devon receive his mortal remains and with it the provision of a financial legacy.[33] Desmond Leslie[34] (Evan's loyal godson) comments (albeit somewhat romantically) that "When Evan realised he was dying of cancer he moved to Buckfast Abbey where he died a heroic death, refusing all drugs and pain killers as a penance for his exotic life style." [35] To the close Evan's love of a good story and the pathos combined in the face of adversity.

Katharine outlived her son by only a few months, moving to a house in London's Belgravia where she was looked after by nurses and a housekeeper.

Almost as soon as Evan died John Morgan (his cousin and penultimate heir) couldn't wait to get his clutches on the Morgan assets. John subsequently (on being handed control of matters by his crippled father, Freddie, the 5th Baron Tredegar) auctioned off Honeywood House, which had been Katharine's home since 1914. Tredegar House was also sold off in 1951.[36]

Long before Evan's final illness Katharine's health was also in decline. Robin Bryans says that in her last years Katharine was "hidden away"[37] at Honeywood.

One heartbreaking portrayal of Katharine, from 1946 claims "she lives in bed in the dark. Her only affection is for a Pekinese..." [38]

With the exception of a short visit to Tredegar House in 1927 (at the time her husband, Courtenay, 3rd Baron, 1st Viscount Tredegar, was President of the National Union of Conservative and Unionist Associations) Katharine and her husband of four decades were estranged. She barely noticed Courtenay's demise in 1934 although flowers were sent to the undertakers at Newport in her name with a card.

Katharine died in London on 4th October, 1949, aged 82 and was cremated. Apart from a few personal gifts and the remnants of her 1890 marriage settlement fund (which was transferred to Evan's Executors, to help reduce his debts) Katharine's final affairs were dealt with by her Carnegie relations. They were also Katharine's choice (in her will) for small legacies and personal items of art and jewellery. 'My ashes shall not be taken to Wales' was also a condition.

Adoration and Mockery of Katharine

Evan Morgan adored his mother. His first book of poetry 'Fragments', is dedicated "TO MY MOTHER". One poem in the selection is 'Verses to my Mother'[39] and exudes incestuous overtones that sit uncomfortably close to Oedipus, describing "a love far greater than any lover knows.....outloving any lover, outloving anyone".

Yet Evan also forever mocked his mother in descriptions he gave of her to his contemporaries. He often revelled in displaying a cruel streak, perfected from an early age, when as a spoilt child he learned he could usually get exactly what he wanted, including attention, by telling the tallest of tales and even deliberately lying.

It is curious that Evan lashed out at Katharine, she was the only parent who took a tiny bit of interest in him, but who in common with all aristocratic Mamas of the age she possessed a somewhat erratic staying power over mothering either of her two offspring, her attention waned speedily, babies and children were solely the territory for wet nurses, nursemaids and nannies to handle. Katharine's sole contribution to mothering was the compilation of a story and picture book entitled 'The Crimson Ducks'[40], dedicated to her son Evan and daughter Gwyneth, a wayward girl who died a horrendous death before she was thirty.[41]

Whilst Evan wrote several poetic verses affectionately dedicated to his mother he often made fun of her, at worse inventing with a nasty, juvenile cut some preposterous tales of her climbing trees, bellowing out Kingfisher-like-calls, and making bird's nests large enough to sit in and coo. Indeed the climax to this was to infer that he was actually born in one of these nests, from an egg.

The bird stories were wicked Evan-made-fantasies, but these were lapped up and strangely believed by some. In fact the claims were based on an innocent pastime of Katharine's (to ease her crippling arthritis) coupled with exaggerating a few alarming episodes from Lady Tredegar's real flights of fancy, into studying religious imagery in paintings.[42] Later she descended into chronic, agitated, mental health, she had an aversion to light, draughts, noise and particularly to her husband, Courtenay and his succession of mistresses.[43]

Sadly these stories of an avian monster created by Evan around Katharine the bird-woman endure even today, and were even more exaggerated by a line of guides at Tredegar House, who since 1973 showed visitors around the old Morgan homestead in South Wales. These anecdotes are silly, viscous and unacceptable, and blight on Katharine's memory. [44]

Even the gullible accept the 'egg laying' fantasy as too ridiculous and logic dictates that a frail lady like Katharine would be unable to weave branches into a nest large enough to sit in, yet the stories persist. Curiously no photographs exist of Katharine's great feats of engineering. The National Trust, the present custodians of Tredegar House are aware of the extravagant tales still being told to visitors about Katharine and are striving to encourage only fully researched information. After all the Morgan family doesn't need invented anecdotes, their real lives were colourful enough.

When Evan was paying the bill for his less well-off drinking cronies at the Randolph Hotel, Oxford, or Café Royal, the Savoy or the Eiffel Tower Restaurants, in London his words were always taken as gospel. Katharine's avian persona found its way into numerous memoirs of Evan's more successful hangers on, most of whom repeated or paraphrased the remarks of the London Society hostess Lady Emerald Cunard [45] when introducing Evan as " This is Mr Evan Morgan, who looks like the poet Shelley [Evan always liked dressing up] and whose mother makes birds' nests." [46] .

One commentator, repeating the comment of "Lady Tredegar ...building, each spring, a nest" [47] added "It was a time of considerable eccentricity amongst the British upper classes." [48]

Despite this mitigation there was a wealth of endearing, kinder testimony about Katharine from Evan's sometime familiar, Aldous Huxley[49] who described Katharine as "a very delightful person" [50] and the woman Evan disastrously attempted to woo, Frances Stevenson [51](later wife of David Lloyd George[52]), who records in her diary in 1919 (after referring to Evan as "very clever but thoroughly degenerate"[53]) about a planned weekend staying with Katharine at Honeywood House, Rowhook "It is a great pity, as Lady T, is devoted to him, [Evan] & she is a dear". [54]

These sentimental and engaging sources of Huxley and Stevenson are excellent material for stories about Evan. However, Evan succeeded in portraying his mother to the outside world as unbalanced. This was in order that he could create greater interest in himself, in a sort of warped way of showing-off to attract followers.

These accounts of Evan's iniquitous take on his mother making bird's nests are in any case discredited once and for all by the truthful, compelling and intriguing description of an occasion when the writer Cecil Roberts [55] went to dine with Evan and Katharine (and others) at the time the Morgan town house was situated at 48, Grosvenor Square,

London. It was here that Roberts discovered the reality of Katharine's hobby of constructing bird's nests.

"After dinner, when coffee had been served in the drawing-room, a footman opened a trestle near Lady Tredegar and put on it a large tray with an assortment of wools, straw, hair, cotton, twigs, moss and leaves.

"You must think it peculiar," she said. "Some women like to do petit-point and needlework- it tries my eyes too much. This is more amusing."

We inquired about the types of nests she made. "Large ones and small ones, some rough and some lined, for different birds. I've had all sorts of tenants!" she replied. "I plant the nests out in the bushes and hidden places. Then I watch. It's better than fishing- getting bird tenants!" She laughed and demonstrated her work. Her fingers were very nimble. She achieved an astonishing verisimilitude.

"Of course, I take my models from real life," she explained." [56]

Roberts' testimony is exactly how Katharine's strange but charming interest in birds' nests should be recalled and celebrated. She was always fascinated (as indeed Evan was with birds and their antics). Still preserved in a garden out-shed at Honeywood House today (now a lavish nursing home) are glamorous reproductions of birds set in stained glass windows.

There may be an element of accuracy in how one friend of Evan's informs another friend about Katharine's endowment to small birds.

"Have you heard that [Evan's] mother has the unusual gift, perhaps the mania, for making chaffinch's nests? She retires for some weeks at a time and then emerges with a perfectly constructed nest which would deceive an ornithologist." [57]

1914-19

More fragments about Evan and his family

Courtenay's War:
1914

Liberty as a Hospital Ship

The outbreak of war one hundred years ago in 1914 led to Evan's father Courtenay offering his magnificent steam yacht *Liberty* to the Admiralty as a hospital ship, a gesture for which he received high praise. [58] A few weeks before war was declared the Morgans entertained Prince Arthur of Connaught [59] -their relative in waiting- for the opening of the extension to the Alexandra Dock in Newport, but the small talk was only of the forthcoming war.

OPENING. NEW. DOCK. BY. PRINCE. ARTHUR.

The event straddled Evan's coming of age which merited only passing reference. [60] Evan had no intention of joining his father on military service, as soon as it was safe to flee, he left Wales with a perfect plan: to study at Christ Church College, in the University of Oxford.[61]

Evan at Oxford

The writer Aldous Huxley [62]who was described in an interview as "the wittiest and most irreverent" [of novelists] " [63] was at Balliol College Oxford and he helped to edit the compilation of University's best verse known as 'Oxford Poetry'; two of Evan's poems appeared in the 1917 compilation.[64] Other contemporaries of Evan in his Oxford days included such figures diversely apart in literary genre as the crime-writer Dorothy L Sayers (Somerville College) and the fantasy guru, JRR Tolkien (Exeter College) who both had poems published in 'Oxford Poetry', alongside Evan.

An earlier literary compilation curiously swept Evan into the list of the glorious dead poets of the Great War, adding "To these we have now to add daily the songs of dead heroes of the type of Charles Sorley, Colwyn Phillips, Evan Morgan and countless others."[65] Evan also makes mention with two works (as the Hon. Evan Morgan 2nd Lieut, Welsh Guards) in 'Soldier Poets : songs of the fighting men.' [66]

Evan's Great War Poetry

Evan at least went into battle with some of his poetry. 'Fragments', his first volume of verse, in 1916, contains heroic poems of war and sacrifice of others by the new 'soldier poet', described, in 1917, as from the same literary set as the late Rupert Brooke". [67] It was not only Evan who made capital out of "the war poetry boom" [68] after Brooke's death in 1915 from blood poisoning. Yet, Evan could not have known "the handsomest young man in England"[69] that well or at all at Oxford (Brooke was in any case a Cambridge man) or shared much time together at Garsington Manor.[70] The closest Evan ever got to "poor Rupert Brooke" [71] was appearing in the same publications of verse about soldier poets of the Great War. Evan failed to be included in the landmark volume 'Georgian Poetry' alongside his dead hero Brooke, despite Evan knowing the book's editor, the influential homosexual, Sir Edward Marsh.[72]

Garsington was the social lubricant for Evan achieving a slight acquaintance with members of the Bloomsbury group, enough to provoke a mocking description from Virginia Woolf of "There was a poet called Evan Morgan in black velvet with a scarlet ribbon and a ruff..."[73] and a jibe from Lytton Strachey that Evan was "a tall bright-coloured youth with a paroqueet nose, and an assured manner, and the general appearance of a refined old woman of high birth"[74]; The latter two literary talents had no time for Evan but a better, albeit unlikely coupling descended into a short companionship between the rich poet-playboy Evan and the intellectual Aldous Huxley, who was a wartime fixture living at Garsington Manor.

Evan's Early Carnal Relationships

Osmond Grattan Esmonde

Front : O S Esmonde, Lois Sturt with Evan

Evidence exists of Evan being the subject of an infatuation by his Oxford contemporary Osmond Grattan Esmonde,[75] an Irish Republican rebel in the years that followed. [76] Evan encouraged the boy, three years his junior on his mad crush.

Evan fancied that it was of the same proportion as Bosie Douglas's fascination for Oscar Wilde. Cyril Hughes Hartmann acted as the go-between. Evan's sweet-talking messages (via Evan's letters to Cyril) include these passages

" Give Esmonde my love and beseech him to write to me. I will at once answer." [77] " ..... remember me to Esmond(e) and say I for one will gladly hail him as a fellow poet, he one by his own toil, by Gods!"[78] and" ...let us turn to other topics, Esmond(e) for instance – what you have written to me, about his feelings for myself, quite naturally pleases, and in so far as he is concerned your intelligence on the matter shall be kept hidden from him."[79] Finally a 'PS' reads "(in red) Love and much more than love, namely admiration, to be given to ESMOND(E) from me........"[80]

Ballynastragh House, Gorey.   Co. Wexford.

Evan spent holidays with Esmonde in Ireland at Ballynastragh House,[81] they rode and fished and walked the countryside together, discussed the pros and cons of the romantic poets and debated the hidden meaning of A E Housman's 'A Shropshire Lad'. This cycle of sixty-three poems, with its importance of desire and seizing the day, besides the author's homosexual undertones was a particular favourite of Evan's.

Kenelm Lister-Kaye

Kenelm

Another boy captivated by Evan was Kenelm Lister-Kaye,[82] dubbed "one more of his early loves".[83] They first came across each other at Eton College. Evan's special attentions in praising the older boy's prowess on the cricket pitch[84] lured him across from sport to join Evan's secret web of oddball confederates including James Lonsdale Bryans,[85] who together with Peter Churchill [86] all indulged in sexual shenanigans and celebrated black mass. These rituals are fully explained in 'Not Behind Lace Curtains: the Hidden World of Evan, Viscount Tredegar.'

Evan insisted that "genius [was] the exclusive domain of practicing male homosexuals". [87] Lister-Kaye was just a year older than Evan and (like Esmonde) the heir to a baronetcy, with connections through his mother to the Dukes of Newcastle and the famous Hope Diamond.[88]

The older boy "worshipped"[89] Evan. However his family (and in particular his straight-lace father) was horrified on "hearing how Kenelm [had failed to get his cricket blue as he] ... was sporting ancient costumes in the black mass with his fellow-Etonian Evan Tredegar. Kenelm succumbed so completely to Evan's spell that [he] was prepared to fight with his father about rejecting the family college at Cambridge University in favour of [Trinity College] Oxford where Kenelm insisted on going in order to be with Evan Tredegar..." [90]

As the Great War ensued Evan and Kenelm joined Oxford's snobs rowing and punting on the Cherwell, sipping champagne on the river bank and later joining daring dandies and swells and Hoorah Henry's entertaining and cavorting in the student sitting rooms and fancy dress parties at the Randolph Hotel. The glittering atmosphere of leisure and pleasure was only interrupted by the latest bulletins from the War Office of the poor sods they knew amongst the dead and wounded in battle.

The Lister-Kaye family "disapproved of Evan's influence over Kenelm and their involvement in the black mass with boys from their Uncle Newcastle's private Choir School..." [91]

When his conscience was pricked Kenelm joined the 3rd Battalion of the West Yorkshire Regiment. He later took up flying, always a consuming interest and went into the Royal Flying Corps (he was later a Squadron Leader in the RAF). He married late in life. In the years that followed the two young lovers became estranged, although saw each other occasionally.

Evan's War Wounds c 1916

Evan and Courtenay

In the wave of even more deaths in battle and from disease of many young British aristocrats in the Great War and to ensure the Morgan family face was saved from adverse comment and shame over Evan's apparent lack of duty in serving his country, he joined the Welsh Guards in 1915. This service is duly recorded in the London Gazette.[92] However the sole evidence of war service is a studio photograph showing the Tredegar heir and his father Courtenay together in their respective military uniforms, marking out Evan masquerading as a soldier, uneasily wearing an ill-fitting soldiers' garb. Soon after the flash from the photographer's gun had vanished, so had Evan, back into civilian togs. He lived out the first years of the Great War flirting, philandering and writing poetry for magazines like *World* [93] and *New Age* [94] as well as speaking " in the Poets Club, at small meetings, at firesides, in studios, in clubs, [and] at raggs (?)"[95]in London and Oxford, albeit downed at times by his troubled health.

Evan and Cyril Hughes Hartmann

On 26th February 1916, Evan wrote to Cyril Hughes Hartmann from Honeywood House: "[I] have just had a severe attack of pleurisy which has started my right lung again, so am on sick leave until the 22nd of March."[96]

Then on 25th July, 1916 he wrote to Cyril from Lyme Regis:

"I have just had a very severe operation for a bad abscess in the left ear and am down here recovering: tis divine...."[97]

Later in 1916 when some new bolstering up of the soldier lie was needed, a report was circulated that Evan " looked fit again after his long convalescence from wounds received in action with the Welsh Guards." [98]

Although Evan's health was erratic, his chronically diseased lungs may not ever have passed him fit for action in the field. In any case, there was a deliberate attempt at covering up his adequacies to serve his King and country and fight. Illness (as some patriots saw it) was a sign of congenital weakness and was not an escape or excuse if one hailed from a family (like the Morgans) who were born to be leaders of men and fighting men.

Evan's father's cousin Leolin Foreister-Walker once said of the Morgan men:

"In their history there was not one melancholy Celt amongst us, not one with that brooding mysticism, as in modern times we have been taught to believe was the inherent quality of Welshmen. They were strong men, fighting men, some thinking men, but all active workers who seemed to find a delight in living." [99]

Both Evan and his father broke the mould albeit no one could fail to notice Evan's 'delight in living'. To some credit his name appears at charity events during the Great War.

At Grosvenor House.

The gayest of all the tables at yesterday's souvenir charity luncheon in Grosvenor House was that occupied by Lady Cunard. She had gathered at it Sir L. Mallet, the Hon. Evan Morgan, Lady Diana Manners, Miss Phyllis Boyd and Miss Nancy Cunard. [100]

Several aristocratic mothers with precious sons asked for strings to be pulled in the War Office. [101] Later the Morgan pretence was mitigated by squeezing Evan into a series of pen-pushing jobs in Whitehall, followed in 1919 with him acting as a 'go-for' with the British Press Bureau at the Paris Peace Conference. [102]

Wherever Evan was in situ as an unpaid civil servant (from 1917-19) he used up large amounts of official government Ministry headed note paper (including some from No 10 Downing Street) writing to friends and showing off his exalted position (signing in red ink) as an 'Hon. Private Secretary'. [103]

In early 1917 he wrote Cyril Hughes Hartmann:

"Forgive office paper but my work is so appalling in its immensity just at present that unless I sent you this line *inter alia* you would never hear from me at all..."[104]

Also in mid 1917 Evan spent time at Cyril's home at Selsey in Sussex [105]where he enjoyed "a peaceful and quiet time...."
[106]

How Cyril found Evan's Visit to Selsey

Evan was not remembered by Cyril as being a particularly good house guest:

"Evan gave more trouble as a guest in a small house (The Thatched House, Selsey) than anyone else I have ever remembered. He would not get up in the mornings and always had to have his hot water bottle renewed several times; he was never in time for meals; he kept me up into the small hours of the morning which was strictly against the seaside summer house at Selsey [which his parents considered to be beneficial]; and he rose in the middle of the night and stopped the clock in the hall by which the whole household ran, because he said its ticking kept him awake. But old Nannie adored him and was ready to put up with it all. This was entirely due to charm on his part, not to snobbishness on hers. Titles meant nothing to Nannie."[107]

Evan's Love of Cyril

Although Evan writes to Cyril as "My Dear Kyrile" [a pet name] and signs the letters with "Love" or "Ever Yours" the correspondence never exposes any evidence that they were lovers. They both suffered from serious lung ailments and exchanged their writings for mutual comment; moreover the letters to Cyril often show a gentler side to Evan. There was high brow talk of literature and art and literary criticism as in this example:

"....when is the new Revolution in Art to come: When the British renaissance? God, let it come soon! Look at us, pity us, wallowing in the foetid [sic] superstition of the archaic laws of the Royal Academy, the precedents laid down by Dickens, Thackeray, Lytton, Tennyson – in all else free save art, and the blasted public are happy, and contented – nay even more delighted bound in their trammels.

The luxuriant Tree of Art with her ever changing blossoms and ever varying leaves has been clipped and trimmed like a yew hedge – however enough is said for now. Spero! I will keep the sketch of the gipsy boy apart for you and will when I feel in the mood do you a better one. "[108]

But between the lines there may have been longings too as in this later letter when Evan writes to Cyril in more personal terms:

"None of those moments of utter friendship was completely realized during their presence, it is only when a certain time has elapsed that they come fully into perspective and each realizes how much more he might have done to have intensified them."[109]

Evan and Cyril shared a greater love for the same man, Evan's cousin Raymond Rodakowski[110], who was killed in the course of the Great War. In June, 1918, writing from Algiers in North Africa (where he was recuperating in a warmer climate) Evan sums up what Oxford and friends he knew in time past meant to him:

"But it is particularly to Oxford that I write, to the places where most I have enjoyed my life, to my companions there, to the shade of my beautiful mistress (Oxford) to your quaint rooms and to the ever beloved memory of Raymond.

Out here it is the essentials that thrust home on the sentiments. Friendship, true, and disinterested, I am beginning just beginning to realise the full value of; and appreciation of one's idiosyncrasies, eccentricities, foibles, faults and fancies and the tender forgiveness of such on the part of those with whom I most come in contact are all to me now most precious things too little treasured before. Earp [Tommy Earp[111]]. Childe [Wilfred Childe[112]] and many another, sunk in the deep grey thoughts of that majestic city of myths and fancies, whose very origin is as obscure as the deeps of the silver stream that nearly encompasses it, begin to rise before me clothed in more radiant apparel, in more glorious raiment, since I more truly understand the full extent of their tolerance to me; and you Kyrile, you have ever risen step by step in the ladder leading to that minute loft, the chamber of mine imaginings, holding there the unique position of tutor and pupil." [113]

1920-25

Evan's self- exile to Cumner, near Oxford c 1920

Rumours about him becoming a monk

Evan had converted to the Roman Catholic faith during the Great War.[114] In 1920, a rumour circulated that he was planning to give up his entire life inheritance and become a monk. This was met with denials and shock from his parents, especially his father, and ridicule from his contemporaries.

When Evan was under pressure he would panic or disappear. From the safety of self-exile in a country cottage on Cumner Hill, near Oxford, Evan (keen to explain how the rumour had arisen) spoke to the Press, eager for a headline.

The comment (that follows) was Evan at his most imaginative and mischievous.

He adored his spot of fame.

"When in America [recently] I lived for two months as a guest of a Jesuit brotherhood in a Franciscan monastery and there I was permitted to live the life of a monk. During this time I was visited by a large number of reporters who asked me why I preferred the secluded life of a monastery to a society life. I answered that I was studying the life of a monk. I was then asked if I was going to be one, and I replied that I could not say but if heaven so willed I would obey. The reporters then published statements that I had become a monk and resigned my birthright. They also added that it was perfectly true since it was even unknown to me."[115]

THE HON. EVAN MORGAN.

Origin of the Monastery Rumour.

DETESTATION OF SOCIETY LIFE.

About this same time to tantalise and tease Evan wrote and published "The Monk's Chant."[116]He addressed this to his Catholic mentor and friend Shane Leslie. [117]

The Monk's Chant - *To Shane Leslie*

O that I might sink
Into that deep pool
Ardent with desire
Of His burning rule,
In his chastening fire
O that I might sink.

O that I might fall
Through the severing clouds,
Into that deep pool
Through sevenfold shrouds:
Ardent for His rule
O that I might fall.

O that I might rest
As a sleeping child
Happy in His hands
To Him reconciled;
O'er the arid sands
O that I might rest.

O that I might weep
Wounded to the heart
Pain in every limb
Tortured every part;
Wounded but by Him
O that I might weep.

O that I might lie
In one precious scar,
Lie as soothing balm
Where I once did mar:
O that I might lie.[118]

Evan the wandering poet

Restored to the life of a wandering poet and not a monk (although he was hankering to study for the priesthood at Beda College, Rome, to further deeper sighs from his father, Courtenay), Evan spent a good deal of time abroad, in Paris and Rome and the Vatican in particular. Such excursions were generally launched with a farewell party. One of these goodbyes is documented:

"A few days before his departure for Rome [where his Catholic cronies in Cardiff had promised him papal honors in exchange for hard cash] Evan gave a party at which a great many of his closest hangers on gathered to say farewell. Among the crowd were Hon. Lois Sturt [who seven years later became Evan's first wife], Mrs Lovat Fraser, Miss Myrtle Farquharson, Mr Stephen McKenna, Miss d' Erlanger, and Mr Ambrose McEvoy."[119]

Of this small group of admirers it is of note that twenty-one year-old Lois Sturt was amongst the party. Evan had known her for several years through his friendship with her brother Gerard, who died at the end of the Great War.[120] Another name to highlight is Ambrose McEvoy, [121] a Society painter and artist, (he painted both Lois and Evan[122]) and many other members of the Bright Young Things.

There were tricky personal issues for the Tredegar heir in the early 1920s including a public fall out with his fellow writer Ronald Firbank (over a book dedication by Ronnie in 'The Princess Zoubaroff[123] followed by a frivolously acid vignette of Evan as 'Hon. Eddy Monteith' in Firbank's' ' The Flower Beneath the Foot' [124]).

These episodes caused Evan's father more anxiety, largely over how others, (in high places) perceived the future shape of the life of the homosexual Lord Tredegar in waiting.

Evan's increased interest in the appeal of the Church of Rome and his contributions to Catholic coffers led to him being made a Papal Knight, but in 1923 he was praised (even by his father) for serving King George V and Queen Mary when they visited the Vatican during an official tour of Italy.

It was a calm of sorts for Katharine. Moreover this period of post war life marks almost the only time Katharine was restored to life and was able to take part in some Society events, even although her estranged husband Courtenay was flaunting his latest mistress.

On 30th January 1921 Katharine wrote to Cyril Hughes Hartmann (who was in Spain to research for a book, he had also spent time there with Evan) :

"I am so glad you are with Evan; it makes all the difference to me to feel he has a staunch friend with him! Tell him – please – that I got his last letter all right; also that I wrote to his father and asked him straight out if he had had a certain visitor staying for the Xmas party. He answered yes – but not quite so shortly as all that! Everyone has a great deal to say about it all, and I am not surprised. But there is nothing to be done, at present.

I am living very quietly but see a fair amount of faithful friends and go to a good many matinées – just to show that I am alive, but not kicking – yet!

I think you must be having a rather nice time, and I envy you considerably, for to be in Spain is a great longing on my part, but I fear impossible just now!" [125]

Evan's house share with wayward sister Gwyneth

DROWNED

HON. GWYNETH MORGAN.
The body of a young woman found in the River Thames near Wapping, was identified by relatives as that of Gwyneth Erica Morgan, daughter of Lord Tredegar. Miss Morgan, who was under medical supervision at the time, slipped from the house during a dense fog the morning of December 11. She wore only pajamas and a woolen dressing gown. Lord Tredegar, one of the wealthiest British peers and well known as a sportsman, offered a large reward.

Hon. Gwyneth Ericka Morgan
(1895-1924)
A Beautiful Nuisance

For several years in the 1920s Evan shared a house in Belgrave Square, Westminster, London,

- 38 -

with his wayward sister Gwyneth, whose body was fished out of the River Thames in 1925. [126]   Here the two of them subscribed to their mutual taste for the bohemian style with literature and art serving as a decoy and staying well away from their father's interests and love of sport and sailing.

Evan (and occasionally Gwyneth) accompanied their mother Katharine to the opera at Covent Garden. [127]   Later Gwyneth's life descended into chaos and finally her disappearance ending in an extreme death in 1925, at the age of twenty-nine. [128]   Evan loved Gwyneth: he kept a red conte drawing of his sister (by Scottish artist Margaret McDonald [129]) in his bedroom at Honeywood House. [130]

Gwyneth's life and death is the subject of the book 'A Beautiful Nuisance'. [131]

Evan in Venice and Rome

1925

In 1943 when Evan was defended at his Court Martial[132] by Sir Walter Monckton, the great advocate declared that his client would be "more at home in a Doge's Palace of the fifteenth century than the present day."   Evan did have a chance to play the Doge's part when his good friend Baroness d'Erlanger [133] spent a year organising a pageant at Venice in 1925/6. Viscountess Wimborne [134] was among the well- known Society women to take part in it. All the participants wore costumes of the fifteenth century with wonderful head dresses and jewels to match. Evan led one of the processions. For a single glamorous day and night the pageant created some of the old splendour of Venice of bygone days.

Whilst many of Evan's contemporaries visited Venice year on year, as he was a notable Catholic convert in the British aristocracy, he much preferred the beauties and treasures of Rome, bodily and those made of ancient stone, including it's glorious Catholic icons, statues, saints and sinners. It was in Rome at the Vatican that Evan was a Papal Knight and Chamberlain of the Sword and Cape from the early 1920s. [135] That said : one Catholic scholar cautions that Chamberlain of the Sword and Cape was not so grand a title as it sounds - it was an honorific title given quite freely to aristocrats and other generous Church] donors."[136]

Pope Pius XI took a personal interest in Evan's case with a "matrimonial essay" [which the Pontiff] unadvisedly bade him try when [Evan's] heart was set on the priesthood. His quaint character stimulated Roman excitement when he entered the Beda College."[137] Spending too much time chasing Italian boys Evan later left his studies (under threat of being expelled, exposed and jailed) and returned to England to pursue a different life path.

However Evan visited Rome almost every year to fulfil his duties as a lay member of the Pope's entourage at least until the new Pope's reign from 1939. Pope Pius XII was less amenable to his Welsh Chamberlain, however Evan's continued his associations with several British diplomats once attached to the Holy See, including Sir Alec Randall [138] and Francis D'Arcy Osborne. [139] These men knew of Evan's twilight world trawling through the streets of Rome and other European cities in search of 'rough trade'. According to one diarist D'Arcy Osborne had a proclivity (albeit described as 'innocent') for young boys. [140]

Besides the high ranking British diplomats looking out for Evan he was (according to Robin Bryans) not unknown to Giovanni Battista Montini,[141] who later reigned as Pope Paul

VI. [142] Evan adored taking part in any lavish ceremony at the Vatican although he had to be content to be a mere witness in the shadows to one ancient ritual when the Pope was "accompanied in grand procession by the flabella, the traditional ostrich feather fans, symbols of royalty going back to the time of the Pharaohs."[143]

A L Rowse on Evan

A L Rowse [144] (author of "Homosexuals in History"[145]) makes no bones of what he thought of the Hon. Evan Morgan: "greatly disapproving" [146] of his life style when he met him once in Rome.

Evan's declaration that the East End of London was "utterly promiscuous and bisexual" [147] could be easily and equally applied to how Evan saw Rome, and the ease by which he conquered his numerous male targets for carnal pleasure in the Eternal City.

Rome was a pleasure dome, a city of sin; Evan always preferred passing his life in Rome other than visiting the famed Italian cities of Venice, Florence and Naples. Of these destinations Evan's admirer Ronnie Firbank found a drain on his travels and pocket and teased Evan about his capture of the street boys thereabouts with their beautiful olive and bronzed bodies and sexual dexterity. The Island of Capri appealed to Evan when he grew tired of Rome. [148]

When Evan converted to the Roman Catholic faith in 1919 he presented some valuable gifts to his local diocese is Wales, he was on very good terms with Francis Mostyn,[149] Archbishop of Cardiff, but favours from that listening post ended on Mostyn's death in 1939.

Evan's erratic health c 1925

In the summer of 1925 Evan had spent a quiet period in Oxford mourning his sister Gwyneth and writing an epic poem "In Pace"[150] to ease his conscience. By the autumn of the year Evan's erratic health was again in the headlines. Reports issued referred to the fact that he had a "slight internal operation…in London [and was] progressing satisfactorily." [151]

In an early news report that same year (by the respected Yorkshire Post) Evan was highlighted as always being "known among his friends for a decided independence of idea and character."[152]

Evan Recuperates in Portugal
With Uncle Lancelot Carnegie

With the dust beginning to settle on Gwyneth's life and death, Evan languished for several months in London and with his mother at Honeywood House. Illness struck him down again, this malady also required an operation and further surgery. When he was well enough he left Britain for a visit to his uncle, the Hon. Sir Lancelot Carnegie[153] (his mother's brother) , who was British Ambassador at Lisbon, Portugal. [154] Evan's recuperation over, he travelled through Portugal and Spain for several months.

1927 onwards

Evan is hit again by Ill-health in the South of France

In 1927, after recovering from the trauma in London over the bogus invitations sent out by practical jokers for his 34th birthday party [155], Evan was holidaying in the south of

France. A lover of the new flying bug that had caught spirit of the age for excitement and danger, he jumped on-board a flight from London to Marseilles.[156] After a prior engagement at Cannes, during which he dined with Pablo Picasso,[157]he later journeyed by road to Juan-les-Pins. Alas, all was not well.

Whilst staying at Juan-les-Pins, he developed a temperature of 103 degrees as a result of serious ear trouble, possibly caused by the air travel. This malady (a recurring problem) required treatment and consultation with a specialist in London.[158]

Evan: The Catholic Poet of the 1920s and 1930s

Other Romps

Alistair Graham   Rosa Lewis

Also in the 1920s Evan came to know Alistair Graham[159]: a minor aristocrat and homosexual. Graham is cited as an Oxford friend and lover of Evelyn Waugh.[160] Alistair stuck around Waugh long enough to take photographs at Barford (the Graham family home [161]) of the famous ' He Evelyn, She Evelyn' (Waugh and his first wife Evelyn Gardner[162]).

From Waugh's perspective, the author of the upper class romp 'Brideshead Revisted'[163] (that waxes and wanes on all that was astonishing, sad, horrific and wasteful about the 'Bright Young Things' brigade) " barely knew " [164] Evan Morgan. [165]

Graham probably first met Evan at the Cavendish Hotel (in London's Jermyn Street[166]), an establishment run by Evan's guardian angel, the "warm hearted" [167] Rosa Lewis [168]. The Cavendish was pride of place for displays of

Evan's raffishness and seedier sexual high jinks. As Evan had permanent rooms there he could come and go as he pleased.

The brief encounter with Graham was around 1927; this led to Graham's short patronage by Evan -and men like Evan- the full depths of the relationships being unclear, but Graham slept around and was seen as a loose cannon.

Increasing labelled insolvent, a dangerous drunkard with a domineering mother, Graham travelled to London and abroad to escape creditors and his Mama's wrath; Evan and Graham's paths may have continued anywhere from Oxford to Paris or Cairo to Constantinople. Graham was enticed by Evan Morgan's plentiful supply of free booze.

As a result (perhaps engineered by entrapment) the full weight of the law governing homosexuals in the 1920s came tumbling down on Alistair Graham. It is alleged that he was caught *in fragranti* with a man in a West End hotel. He is also said (and is in print albeit with no verifiable source) that *Evan* was the other man in this homosexual scandal. [169]

In any case Graham's capture resulted in his rapid exile abroad. [170] He was smuggled into the British diplomatic corps and served in Greece and North Africa. Later he removed himself to New Quay in West Wales where in 1936 he bought a house and later (through the circle of Augustus John) became a friend of Dylan Thomas .[171]

Like Sebastian Flyte the anti- hero of 'Brideshead Revisted' (the character is partially based on Graham, and it is said that Alastair's name was mistakenly substituted for Sebastain's several times in the original manuscript).

Graham has been resurrected in further fictionalised accounts of his life and times (and some people have fallen for the fiction as fact in each case). Assertions such as that he was " extremely well connected , with friends in government and the royal family." [172] - thus one would have thought (like Evan) he would have escaped from his offences scot-free. It also, rather regrettably, remains only fiction that Graham's " bacchanalian house parties were a gay assortment of London friends, so much so that his mansion became known locally as Bugger Hall." [173]

During the era of his raucous house parties Evan would have adored to see 'Bugger Hall' over the entrance way to Tredegar House.

Marquerites, Off Cannes

Another of Evan's monastic retreats

At about the same time as another health blip, Evan was given   a pass by   the Pope   to enter   the restricted Monastery on the Island of Marquerites,   off Cannes. Almost certainly this was also suggested as a place of retreat and inner contemplation since the Tredegar heir had been counseled by the Holy Father to look to marriage as he was not cut out for the priesthood. By the end of the 1920s the Abbot of Marquerites decided to stop all new novitiates, not because of any hanky-panky by Evan, but as the French government had plans to purchase the site for a casino. [174]

Once the pretty Island with lovely scenery , beautiful woods and perfect bathing was privately owned by a Cistercian order, these monks had also once owned substantial territories around Cannes, Mougins and Vallauris. Today, the island is mainly owned by the town of Cannes although part of it is still privately owned; the monks occupy the smaller adjoining island of St Honorat Island.

Throughout his life Evan sought refuge in Catholic monasteries and sects, notably at Oxford, as well as within the dioceses covered by the Cardinals of Westminster and the Archbishop of Cardiff and the Bishop of Llandaff.

Closest to his heart and soul was Buckfast Abbey, where Evan was ultimately laid to rest in the Abbey's small Private Cemetery, in 1949. The headstone is modest in comparison to others simply stating:

' Of your charity pray for the soul of Evan Frederic Morgan, Viscount Tredegar of Tredegar Park Newport Monmouthshire. '

Whatever his politics or the state of his regular living, the "Hon. Evan Morgan was by nature a mystic; and the fold of the Roman Church was his natural refuge.." [175] As a young man he adored pageantry, it appealed to his inner longing to be someone else, invariably this was a great hero from the pathways of history, a monarch, a Welsh Prince, or brave warrior knight.[176] His tenure as a Papal Knight ensured that for two weeks each year from the early 1920 until 1939 he fulfilled his duties in the Vatican as a Chamberlain of the Cape and Sword.

London Night Club Raided and Evan Was There

Chez Victor

In the early hours of Saturday 12th November, 1927, about twenty strangers, all men, motored up in five cars to the premises of Chez Victor, a luxurious Night Club in London's Grafton Street. They entered the Club in pairs moved up the outside steps, deposited their coats and hats in the cloak room, marched up to the tiny ballroom and sat down at the tables. Dancing was in progress, semi-filled champagne glasses littered the tables.

Outside other men staged a faked motor car collision. The Club doorman hastened to where the collision had taken place to ask if he could help, whilst a further group of men slipped through the unguarded door.

With timings synchronised exactly, the mysterious strangers (who were all really policemen) swooped down from inside and outside upon the throngs of illegal drinkers in Chez Victor, one of London's smallest, but select night clubs.

Police whistles drowned out the sound of saxophones playing, whilst the swarm of detectives faultlessly dressed in full evening wear with red poppies in their button holes revealed their true identities. The policemen proceeded to take the names and addresses of all those present in the Club.

In the period after Evan's return to London, from Rome and the South of France in 1927, and his sham marriage to Lois, he much enjoyed the indulgences of London night life, like Chez Victor, or dropping in at the Cavendish Hotel (where Evan had a key) and then going on to explore the Capital's club land.

One compilation records this brief digest of the notable London clubs frequented by the Bright Young People:

"The Café de Paris has a ballroom that is an exact replica of the dining saloon of the doomed ship Lusitania. It was impossible to dance around the floor without rubbing at least half-a-dozen noble shoulders. It is famous too for an Hawaiian band, and chic posies from Paris, which light up when the lamps are lowered and transformed the ballroom into a kaleidoscopic fairyland of soft music and winking lanterns. After midnight Layton and Johnstone croon of old-fashioned homesteads. Another club is the Piccadilly, where the world dances to Jack Hylton's band. There are jugglers here too and singers of plantation melodies, and Miss Sophie Tucker. Next is the Embassy, where the smiling Lugihi welcomes most crowned heads of Europe, and Dukes and Duchesses are as plentiful as the waiters who glide velvet footed hither and thither to minister to the wants of, those whose names are household words. Then comes Chez Victor where there is the smallest dance floor in the world, and the cream walls are decorated by a famous Italian countess whose hobby is art. Another fashionable club is Ciro's, in Orange Street, which is the nearest thing to Paris in London. Next is the Kit Kat at the top of the Haymarket, famous for its food, lighting, and terribly expensive drinks and where celebrities jostle each other ceaselessly on the tiny floor, and great ones buy steaming kippers at five shillings a pair and attack them with the zest of their chauffeurs in charge of their glistening limousines, which pack the mews outside."

Aside from the attraction of the Embassy Club (where Evan was sure to run into his Royal cousins) there was Gargoyles, in Soho, run by the Hon. David Tennant. [177]

But Evan's chief watering-hole in London, was Chez Victor, [178] an exclusive establishment in Grafton Street, ran by Victor Perosino, an Italian emigrant. For several years the Club reigned supreme, then hit hard times but a transformation into a restaurant brought back some of its old customers. The attraction was that patrons could drink till late and after hours, which broke the alcohol licence regulations. Patrick Kinross observes of the era "People resigned themselves to the fact that night life was a crime and preferred to take an open risk of being caught." [179]

The year that Chez Victor was raided was at the demise of the members' only dance, dining and gaming clubs before many of them changed over to more public establishments, since members were inclined to dodge paying their annual subscriptions, particularly as more clubs sprung up and word got round of their existence.

Chez Victor regularly commissioned the latest cabaret singers, the black pianist 'Hutch' (Leslie Hutchison) being one such act at the time. The Club was frequented by Royalty, aristocracy, politicians, stage and film stars. More ominously, there were reports that the Club was a front for illegal drugs trafficking, especially for supplying cocaine to members of the gentry and the Royal family. [180] some reported that Victor was a dangerous drug pusher. [181]

In November, 1927 in the raid of the Club seventeen people were arrested, including the Hon. Evan Morgan of Queen's Gate.[182] The drinks curfew from twelve (midnight) ran until day break.[183] The Police had been watching the Club for several months. Officers had visited after midnight and been served drinks.

The Hon. Evan Morgan Evan appears as one of those summoned as a 'consumer'. By a fluke he is partly disguised by a typographical error, being shown by the name of "Thetton Evan Morgan." On the night of the raid he was almost certainly entertaining the two men staying at the Cavendish Hotel. Fines varying from £5 to £10 were imposed at Marlborough Police Court on those pleading guilty to consuming liquor after hours. [184]

The Club owner, Victor Perosino summoned on ten separate counts, four for supplying drink after hours and six for offences against Customs and Excise) pleaded guilty to supplying drink after hours and other infringements and was fined £200 and £60 costs.[185]

THE CONSUMERS. /

The following were summoned as consumers :—

RAYMOND PHILLIPS, Down Grange, Basingstoke, and Conservative Club, St. James's-st., S.W

KATHLEEN DUNVILLE, South Eaton-place.

MRS. CHRISTINE WALKER, Harcourt House, Cavendish-sq., W.

IVY HELLIER, Windsor-mans., off Baker-st.

CHARLES M. BUCKLEY, Brompton-sq., S.W.

VERNA JOHNSON, Devonshire House, Piccadilly, W.

THETTON EVAN MORGAN, Queen's-gate, S.W.

DAVID LOWE, Holland Park, W.

CLEMENT JESSELL, Clarges-st., W.

PATRICK SMITH, Gloucester-place, W.

COL. WILFRED EGERTON, Connaught-sq., W.

NIGEL SEELEY (or SMITH), Cavendish Hotel, Jermyn st., W.

JOHN JAMES RAMSDEN, Cavendish Hotel, W.

GIOVANNI GREGORINI, South Eaton-place.

LADY MARION CAMERON, North-gate, Regent's Park, N.W.

COL. GETHING, White's Club, St. James's-st.

MARJORIE HUGHES ONSLOW, Pall Mall, S.W., and Laggan, Ballantrae, Ayrshire.

ERIC RICE, Hertford-st., W.

Above : How One American Newspaper reported the story
of Scotland Yard's consideration for the Prince of Wales.

Although Evan was caught and punished, the Club's best
known patron, accustomed to making visits after midnight
was Edward, Prince of Wales. Scotland Yard planned the
raid that lifted Evan with great precision knowing that the

Prince was elsewhere. Several newspapers in America covered the story of "How the Prince of Wales Was Let Out of the Society Nightclub Raid."

Evan dined out on his arrest for months afterwards, and how the newspapers had covered up his name.

However not even the heir to the throne could save Chez Victor being closed and its owner banished.

In April, 1928, Perosino was deported from Britain by the Home Office, in part under the craze of the hard line policy of Home Secretary, Sir William Joynson-Hicks. Victor was an alien, he had broken the law, that law would not be compromised. Others who had broken the same law (like Kate Meyrick, Society hostess, owner of the '43 Club' at 43 Gerrard Street, Soho) had also been imprisoned.[186]

But deportation was harsher than prison for Victor, the fact was that he had lived for fifteen years in Britain, he married in London [187] and had two children born there.

Victor's appeal to the Home Office over the deportation ruling with others making personal representations to Joynson-Hicks fell on deaf ears, despite the fact that the same Sir William Joynson-Hicks had himself been " the subject of much chaff.... when he was once found present at the [outlawed] Kit Kat Club when champagne was auctioned for charity after hours."[188]

Victor settled in Paris where he opened a further Night Club, also called Chez Victor. In addition to being a well-known figure in London (where he was occasionally allowed permission to return for short trips to see his children who remained for a while in Britain[189]) Victor continued successfully in the Night Club - Restaurant business in

Paris and elsewhere in France. He was a regular visitor to Le Touquet (where he first went in despair after deportation, he feared any return to his native Italy, under Mussolini).

Victor was a favourite and confidante of many at the playboy resort, in Le Touquet the haunt of many of his old Chez Victor rich and Royal patrons, including the Prince of Wales' sect and the Hon. Evan and Hon. Mrs Evan Morgan.

1928

Engagements, Marriages and the Aftermath

Society Engagements and Marriage

London Agog over Recent Engagements followed by Spate of Mad Marriages

Evan and his first wife the Hon. Lois Sturt followed a trend, a spate of Society engagements that left London agog followed by a spate of mad marriages by homosexual men. These ill- match unions (doomed from the start) were the sole source of conversation at every lunch and dinner party, London's parlours were buzzing with unanswered questions about all these madcap affairs.

At the Café de Paris, the rendezvous for everyone that was chic, smart and elegant, Evan was collared by blood sucking dowagers (whilst dining with his cousin, Princess Arthur of Connaught). He said his lips were sealed. Princess Arthur's husband as well as her sister Lady Maud Carnegie (another of Evan's cousins) were part of the crowd at the opening of the new Mayfair Hotel. They were also tight lipped about the new matrimonial dues, in particular that of Evan and Lois's union.

Gavin Henderson

Whilst the back room fixers were matching and avoiding questions about Evan and Lois, the Welsh Lord and Lady Kylsant's daughter Hon. Honor Chedworth Philipps [190] announced her engagement to Alexander Gavin Henderson [191] a highbrow homosexual and grandson and heir of Lord Faringdon. In April 1927, Gavin returned to London from a romp in Australia and joined his intended to rejoice in the news about his friends Evan and Lois. The Henderson wedding was later held on 2 June, 1927 at St Margaret's, Westminster by the Archbishop of Wales. In the preceding evening the prankish Henderson held a farewell bachelor party at Phyllis Court, Henley. " [192] The proceedings there, with about 30 of Henderson's chums got completely out of control, when 20 gallons of petrol in buckets was thrown on to the Thames and set alight. This was an act of revenge as part of a hoax against Henderson which had taken place a few years before.

One report states: "….. flames leapt up the Cromwellian Wall, burning off the roses for which it is famous, scorching the lawn, and burning the chestnut trees which stand in the grounds….. The wall, which was damaged is of historic value because it was built by Cromwell to protect Phyllis Court against the Royalists. When the fire had died down [Henderson and his friends] returned to their cars and went back to town." [193] The committee of Phyllis Court demanded action against Henderson. Although four summonses were issued by the Conservators of the River Thames and Henderson appeared before Henley on Thames Magistrates Court the case was dismissed as it proved impossible to identity who had ordered the petrol. Henderson's story that he did not go to the garage, did not order the petrol, and did not know that anyone else had done so was accepted, as was the claim that Henderson was on the bank at the time the petrol was set alight and that he could have had nothing to do with it. In presenting evidence of the tomfoolery it merged that Henderson had paid the bill for the evening's mirth of £105, which apparently included the petrol. [194]

Ned Lathom

Ned at war - Xenia painted by Ambrose McEvoy

Next in the mad marriage stakes was the homosexual playwright peer, Edward (Ned) George Bootle Wilbraham, 3rd Lord Lathom. [195] A kindred spirit of Evan, they had known each other intimately at Eton and Christ Church, Oxford. A few years before Ned had escaped an engagement to Irene Curzon, one of the daughters of the famous Indian Viceroy, Lord Curzon. [196] He was a close friend and patron of Noel Coward and (like Evan) on sleeping terms with Ivor Novello.

One retrospective records "The good Earl [Lathom] was Noel Coward's first patron but lived the good life, spent the family fortune and was considered to be a rather risque gay aristocrat". [197] Tales reverberated across the Atlantic of Ned's encounters with hotel bellboys, on his tour of

America in 1923 and (later famously emulated by his intimate chum Noel Coward) Ned was interviewed by newsmen in his hotel room wearing only a dressing gown. [198] Equally lurid were rumours of Ned's frolics with bucking bronco's when he visited a ranch in Alberta, Canada, in enquiries about a business venture (like that of his Eton and Evan contemporary Lord Rodney[199]) where his late father invested large sums of money.[200]

Ned sold off his 11,000 acre land mineral estate and family piles of Lathom House and Blythe House at Ormskirk in Lancashire in 1923, Blythe was a place with its own swimming pool and Turkish baths, and where the no holds barred Earl lavishly entertained all comers but four years later "adopted the wise course of being married at 12 o'clock in the morning thus making it possible for the reception to be held much earlier than usual." [201] Unlike the titled wives to be of Evan and Gavin Henderson, Ned's bride was a divorcee, a shop girl and part time actress named Mrs Xenia Morison.[202] The new Earl and Countess of Lathom described as " twin souls"[203] were married quietly on 2nd June, 1927 and afterwards held a reception for close friends at the Ritz Hotel. Xenia worked with Ned at his tiny furniture shop under the name of Fearnley Ltd, in Davies Street, Mayfair. [204] The honeymoon was a tour of Europe including Norway, Sweden and Germany. Xenia turned her husband's money into starting a dressmaking enterprise to rival that of Lady Bridget Paget's Grafton Street business (where fifty girls were employed) but even with the inducement of offering the latest perfumes from Paris the gamble failed.

Ned's early death - in 1930- at the age of just 34, was in part attributed to the affect of him serving in the Lancashire Yeomanry in the Great War, and he had been in France and Gallipoli and Palestine. [205] The official cause of death was tuberculosis; like Evan, Ned suffered from bad genes, both these men's lives were dotted with crippling illness and frequent operations. Nonetheless this did not dampen either's sex life.

Evan Engaged to Hon. Lois Sturt

Within a few weeks of returning to Britain from his retreats and foreign pilgrimages it was announced in December 1927 [206] that Evan was to become engaged to Hon. Lois Sturt, the daughter of the deceased 2nd Lord Alington of Crichel, Dorset. The coupling of the pair was by arrangement, one of convenience, both parties were bohemian types. Evan's weakness was for picking up boys, Lois (seven years younger than Evan) was an ex- mistress of several of the Royal Princes and had only ended a long standing affair with Reginald Herbert, 15th Earl of Pembroke and Montgomery. The would-be-betrothed had known each other over several years, Lois' brothers Gerard and Naps were close chums of Evan, especially Gerard, who died as a result of massive injuries sustained in the Great War, in 1918. Naps (Napier) was Lord Alington, a faun-like creature, good looking and bisexual. Evan, Lois and Naps were also involved in politics in London's East End where the Morgans and the Sturts were both slum landlords and extensive landowners in Shoreditch, Limehouse and Bow. At the time of his engagement Evan was prospective Conservative party candidate for Limehouse, Lois and Naps were standing for the London County Council. They were all limelight-seekers, and appeared in the many news and gossip columns of the era, their fads and frolics were well catalogued as leading members of the Bright Young People. Lois was famed too as an artist (painter) and actress. She once drove her car so fast through Regent's Park on one of the crazed 'treasure hunts' (a popular pastime for the Bright Young People) that the Police intervened.

SEQUEL TO NEW SOCIETY GAME.

———

The Hon. Lois Sturt, of 38 Portman Square, Marylebone, London, who gained third place in the new society game of "chasing clues" on May 21, was summoned at the Marylebone Police Court yesterday for exceeding the 20-mile speed limit in the Outer Circle, Regent's Park, for driving her car at a speed dangerous to the public, and for failing to stop at the request of a police constable.

The representatives of the law would not accept Lois' explanation that she was following up a clue as a justification for the speed of her car. Lois was fined for speeding.

In May 1926 Lois killed a pedestrian, Arthur George Lewis (aged 46) on the road whilst speeding. At the time she stated that she was on O.M.S.[207] work and had just dropped other workers off when the incident occurred. The verdict was 'accidental death'.

Dinner Party Staged by Sir Arthur and Lady Colefax to celebrate the engagement

On 19[th]December, 1927, London Society folk blessed the engagement of Evan and Lois at a dinner party staged by Sir Arthur and Lady Colefax.[208] The function, originally planned to allow London toffs to meet the actress Miss Ruth Draper was taken over by the wave of celebrations and congratulations to the happy couple, who in effect were the most ineligible of bachelor and spinster. [209]

Evan and the Persecution of Roman Catholics in Mexico.

Evan's protestations over the plight of Roman Catholics in Mexico, that culminated in a long letter to the Daily Express, brought him into favour with literary giants like Grahame Greene.[210] A roaming British born journalist named Francis McCullagh[211] includes a mention of Evan's Mexican campaign in a book about the persecution of Catholics in Mexico in the 1920s, under President Calles. [212]

McCullagh reveals how this came about during the time that the wedding of Evan and Lois Sturt was the most talked about subject in London.

"The Hon. Evan Morgan, the son and heir of Viscount Tredegar, was about to be married, and one day a girl reporter from the Daily Express called on him to get some details of his fiancee's trousseau. Mr. Morgan, who is a sincere Roman Catholic, promised to give her all the information she wanted on condition that she got something into the Daily Express about the persecution in Mexico.   Finally this London newspaper approached the subject with great trepidation and circumspection...." [213]

This was one of Evan's finest hours of achievement as the story of murder and firing squads and American collusion in Mexico was largely ignored by the British newspapers and covered up by the Americans ones.

London Thrills To Engagement of Peer's Son

The deceit over the engagement between Evan and Lois turned to thrills as their friends and enemies predicted a farce, others a disaster. There was an element of both. Evan was aged 34, Lois 27, both were unsuited to living together. The Illustrated London News commented:

"This latter pair [Evan and Lois] have for long been so well known in Society, and so long regarded as leaders in all kinds of ... Mr. Morgan, the only son of Lord Tredegar, has crowded many enthusiasms into his thirty-four years of life, and found many ways of expressing....." [214]

After the very lavish wedding at the Brompton Oratory (which necessitated Lois becoming a Roman Catholic, in a role she prepared for much the same way as she handled a part in film or on stage) the Morgans hardly ever lived together. After vast sums of money were spent on a matrimonial home, blazing rows (public and private), Lois found a house called 'Mumpumps' in Surrey where she indulged her passions for flying [215], horse racing, breeding dogs and continued her love affairs with older men.

Evan Returns again to Oxford

Evan was ejected as an undergraduate at Oxford University and never took a degree, let alone attend at lectures when he was a student, in the years 1914 onwards), once telling his friend Cyril Hughes Hartmann "No(w) Oxford (h)as cast me off, rightly punished me for my behaviour towards it when there. "[216]

However Evan sought sanctuary among Oxford spires in Catholic seminaries (offering respite) and remained a regular face at Oxford romps, parties, functions and literary celebrations, under the auspices of the Catholic Poetry Society. Later, Evan became a respectable member of the Royal Society of Literature. Alfred Noyes, [217] Lord Alfred Douglas [218] and several of the next wave of dilettantes like Chips Channon [219] (whom Evan had coaxed into enrolling himself at Oxford University, a few years earlier [220]) enjoyed Evan's attentions, hospitality and patronage. Evan sneaked his way from time to time into the bedroom of his one time protégé Chips Channon, enough for him to be included in a fabulous mural of several dozen of Channon's friends by the artist John Spencer Churchill.[221]

Later the Evan clique with Channon " darting in and out"[222] included " a whole group [of closeted homosexuals] around [Lord] Mountbatten-[223] [Princes'] Paul of Yugoslavia,[224] Paul of Greece[225] and various others". [226]

Evan always had a roaming eye for the new, emerging generation of Oxford undergraduates. Whenever there was a special occasion afoot Evan's presence (and occasionally his patronage) would be offered. In 1929 Evan's name is unsurprisingly linked to an outrageous event dubbed "the largest cocktail party ever given" [227]. This was staged by joint hosts Hon. Hamish Erskine [228] and his friend, Peter Watson [229] (each like Evan, a predatory homosexual). It began with a lunch, to which Evan was invited, with others [230]and continued all day. The scene (in the University rooms of undergraduates Erskine and Watson) heaved and swelled all day "every minute large motor cars[arriving] full of Bright Young People "with passengers to off load."

Evan Morgan FZS and FRSL

In programmes - for instance at the 1929 Derby Dinner (held on the eve of the horse race) - Evan flaunted two of his less well known titles amongst fellow guests. FZS (Fellow of the Zoological Society) and FRSL (Fellow of the Royal Society of Literature). These were thought curious distinctions to be mentioned in connection with a sporting dinner. [231]

More on Evan and Politics : Evan's Political Targets

Evan's critical comments often without thinking things out got him into trouble. He found himself the centre of a monumental row regarding his comments about Canada on a Parliamentary tour of the country, in 1929.[232] Evan commented that " the region he visited in Canada was not ready to receive settlers from Britain, as this area, the Peace River country, lacked saloons, cinemas, clubs, and other amenities" [233] Canadians rose up to say that saying Evan had " either learned very little about Canada, or not to have understood very well what he did learn."[234]

The Devil rather than Rothermere

Following Evan's defeat at the parliamentary seat of Stepney, Limehouse, he became the prospective Conservative candidate for Cardiff Central. He was widely reported about his dislike for Lord Rothermere (famous as the proprietor of the Daily Mail.) At one speech at a Conservative fete near Newport Evan pitched in his opinion that "he would rather the devil led the Conservative Party than Lord Rothermere." [235] Following personal appeals by Stanley Baldwin and his father, Courtenay Tredegar, Evan stood down at Cardiff in favour of the National Labour candidate, Sir Ernest Bennett. [236]In effect Evan retired from politics later that year 1931. On the death of his father three years later, Evan took his seat in the House of Lords, as the 2nd Viscount Tredegar, he attended only from time to time, but to his credit he led a campaign (by Private Member's Bill) to outlaw the use of gin traps by estate owners.

Evan as Part of the Royal Fixtures and Fittings

Evan (far right) in the company of Queen Mary (centre)

Having spent a month of 1931 taking the waters at Bath (to ease his congested lungs) Evan headed back to his London home at 40, South Street, Park Lane. Evan then off flew to Paris, returning to Britain in May to attend a conference for the organisations representing Commercial Travellers in the country, where he showed an interest, especially as he was President of the United Kingdom Commercial Travellers Association . He was determined to try to have the Prince of Wales act as patron for these workers.[237]

Later Evan went north in the autumn of 1932 to the Highlands of Scotland. In September he was with his Carnegie cousins at Elsick House, Kincardineshire, when they were visited by Queen Mary, where a photograph survives, with a newspaper cutting that explains why Queen Mary was present.

Edinburgh Evening News Thursday 22 September 1932

QUEEN VISITS FRIENDS

TREE-PLANTING CEREMONIES IN NORTH

In October, 1932 Evan also appears in the company of HRHs Prince and Princess Arthur of Connaught at the Mar Lodge gathering. Evan's house party also included, Royal physician Sir Russell and Lady Wilkinson and Colonel and Mrs Spigat Moodie. [238]

MAR LODGE BALL.

A ball was given at Mar Lodge on Monday night by their Royal Highnesses the Prince and Princess Arthur of Connaught.

The Prince and Princess were present with the members of the house party; Colonel Spigat Moodie and Mrs Moodie, Sir R. Wilkinson and Lady Wilkinson, and the Hon. Evan Morgan.

Evan and his appearances at The Spread Eagle at Thame

JOHN FOTHERGILL

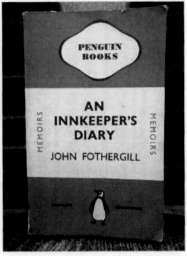

From 1922 to 1932 John Fothergill,[239] a blunt speaking 'author, wit, raconteur and amateur innkeeper' (according to the plaque outside) was the proprietor of The Spread Eagle at Thame, near Oxford. He transformed this into a Mecca for the rich and literary; Augustus John, George Bernard Shaw and HG Wells amongst them. He alienated the locals and had a reputation as an outrageous snob. He also wrote 'An Innkeeper's Diary', a daily record of the characters and shenanigans during his tenure. But anecdotes were cleverly exaggerated for comic or dramatic effect.

From the "Diary" comes a couple of stories about Evan Morgan taking his entourage to this famous pub in the 1930's :

As usual Evan was paying!

"Evan Morgan comes with his usual big party to dinner. He pays for the meal and does all the talking. That's not fair. Since becoming a politician he seems to have lost the romantic and ascetic that he used to have. He leaves his priceless fur coat in our office and brings all his friends to pile theirs – it's his welcome prerogative, for he used to come here in our simple days as well as his.

But tonight when one of them came in to get his cigarettes, I couldn't help asking him if he minded my eating my supper in his cloak-room."[240]

Evan also exercised his prerogative in another visit of bringing along one of his pet birds:

"A wet Sunday and with seating for 60 we lunched 103 plus 11 chauffeurs. Evan Morgan said he'd never seen so many people in so small a place. He didn't make it any better himself by bringing down his Australian crow which ran amok and pecked girls' ankles, having first laid an egg upstairs on his dressing table."[241]

Evan and the Birds

Many stories circulate about Evan's succession of pet birds. The cutting below provides some information about the same period as he was a regular at the Spread Eagle at Thame. [242]

Cyril Hughes Hartmann's tale of Evan's talents with birds

Another earlier tale (from 1917) gives great insight into Evan's peculiar avian skills. Cyril describes a visit (for lunch) to his neighbour Archie Hamilton:

"Evan, who was staying with me, and I had been invited to luncheon and, when we arrived, we found the whole place in a state of consternation. One of Archie' peacocks had strolled into the orangery and perched itself in the middle of the dinner service (the Hamilton crested dinner service which was displayed in the Orangery). Cajolements and corn had been strewn before it, but nothing would induce it to emerge, and every time Archie or anyone else approached it, however cautiously, there was an ominous fluttering as it showed every sign of putting up a stout resistance with claw, wing and tail. Without a moment's hesitation Evan walked nonchalantly into the Orangery and made a kissing noise with his lips at the peacock, which immediately hopped onto his outstretched forearm and came out with him. He afterwards explained to Archie that he did not dare to hesitate even for a moment to ask his permission to try the experiment. Evan certainly did know all about birds."[243]

PIPING CROW LATEST PET OF EVAN MORGAN

The Hon. Evan Morgan, who says he has a sixth sense with animals, has trained a new bird to replace his black and yellow hangnest "Mat." Mat was a celebrated bird and a friend of royalty, prime ministers and home secretaries, Lord Brentford having been a particular favorite of his.

The new bird, an Australian piping crow and very rare, has been christened "Comic," and although it is of a rather vindictive nature, it has taken a strong liking to its owner. It whistles tunes, pecks at strangers and picks up and repeats after its own fashion phrases of letters. He is allowed to fly out of the window whenever he wants, for, though he flies to the top of the highest trees, he will return to Mr. Morgan's shoulder directly he is called.

HIS HOBBY.—The Hon. Evan Morgan, son of Lord Tredegar, with one of the birds he keeps in an aviary at his flat at Kensington.

Godfather Evan and Desmond Leslie

On Thursday 21ˢᵗ July 1921 Evan became a godfather to Desmond Leslie, the infant son of Mr and Mrs Shane Leslie. The christening took place at the Hospital of St John and Elizabeth, St John's Wood. Countess Beatty was chosen as godmother and Lady Leslie, Lady Constance Leslie and Katharine, Lady Tredegar were among others present. [244]

The infant grew up to be "mildly eccentric". One retrospective referring to Evan - records :

"Throughout his life, Desmond maintained a reputation for unconventionality - hardly surprising when one of his godparents was a noted Satanist who kept a pet parrot in his trousers. Desmond Leslie more than matched this behaviour: one of the most popular items on YouTube is a BBC broadcast showing him punching the critic Bernard Levin on live television more than forty years ago."

It is a great pity that a recent book on Desmond Leslie [245] (that contains this quote, above) falls down dramatically on account of it relying almost entirely on the more absurd, oddball elements of Evan's persona from sources that are fanciful and phony and discredited.

Desmond Leslie's letters to Tredegar House during the 1970s are more representative of fact, these excel on showing exactly how much he appreciated Evan's role as godfather and adult mentor. From this cache comes the following fragment recalling the end of 1930s:

"At 14, and at a Catholic monastery school, I didn't even know what gays were...People raised eyebrows at my being there, and took my mother to task for allowing me to visit this scandalous house. But I was totally safe. Evan had passed the word that if anyone as much as touched his godson..he was out, out out…"[246]

Desmond's letters bulge with memories of Evan and guests playing a game called ' In The Manner of the Word' [247] and singing songs to Evan sometimes until two in the morning with " Evan conducting with Blue Boy [Evan's bird, a Hyacinth Macaw parrot [248]] perched on his head contributing an occasional squawk."[249]

"When there was a very large house party we would overflow into the Brown Drawing Room, where a superb Blutner grand piano once stood by the window at the door to the Gold [Gilt] Room."[250]

The last memory Desmond had of visiting Tredegar House paints a sadder picture of decay and the end of an era :-

"My last visit to Tredegar with my bride was shortly after the war [Second World War[251]] . Though owning half the coalfields in South Wales Evan like everyone else, was strictly rationed. (You can image his comments!) We scraped around in his tiny coal bin and gathered just enough for one small fire after dinner in the drawing room, where we huddled in our scarves and overcoats." [252]

Evan was proud to attend Desmond's wedding, prouder still of being present for the christening of Desmond's son Sean, in 1947 - as can be seen in the picture below.

Evan (left) with his godson Desmond Leslie and family

Evan's Lawyer and Mr Fixer

Albert M Oppenheimer, sometime Evan's solicitor was a British subject, born at Frankfurt-on -the-Main, Germany in the 1870s. [253] He died in London, in 1945, aged seventy-three. [254]

Oppenheimer was far from honest. He was fined a large sum by the High Court in a controversial company fraud case in the early 1930s. Despite this defalcation Evan sought representation by Oppenheimer's firm in 1935 in an altogether shady case brought against a Robert Gregory for the theft of Evan's father's cuff links. [255]

Evan also used Oppenheimer to protect him from arrest in a scandal that was carefully covered up regarding Evan and two young men, a 20-year-old valet and 21-year-old seamen, whom Evan had entertained all night at the Cavendish Hotel. One of the men William Goodwin tracked Evan down to his bachelor flat in Charles Street, Mayfair and (along with the other man that Evan had seduced) attempted to blackmail the Tredegar heir. The Police arrested Goodwin and his accomplice and both were jailed for "loitering in Mayfair with intent to commit a felony". [256]

Later in 1943 Oppenheimer's firm also acted for Evan in the proceedings brought by Evan's second wife Princess Olga for divorce. Albert Oppenheimer is cited as being the go between for a number of Lord Alfred (Bosie) Douglas's friends who raised sums to pay the rent on Bosie's Brighton flat.

Evan in California

In the early 1930s Evan was in Riverside, California and a guest of Frank A Millar[257] the proprietor of the Mission Inn hotel.

Evan's visit made such an impact that it features in a book published about Frank Millar and the Mission Inn:

"There was the incident of the visit of the Honorable Evan Morgan, son of Baron Tredegar of England.

Mission Inn : Evan and the Cross of St John

Depiction of John of the Cross Crucifixion

Tall stories are told that Evan acquired a piece of the ' true cross' on which Christ was crucified. In fact the *real* story relates to a reliquary of St John on the Cross at Mission Inn.

" Mr Morgan had arrived at the Inn on a trip around the world. Wandering among the crosses of the collection, he came upon a reliquary of St John of the Cross. Mr Morgan's Catholic sympathies were pronounced, and St John was his patron saint; he went to curator, saying that he wished to buy this cross. The curator told him courteously that nothing in the cross collection was for sale.

"I must buy it." the Honourable Evan Morgan repeated. " You must let me buy it."

Impressed by the absence of any mention of price or inclination to bargain, Mr Borton, the curator promised to lay the matter before Mr Miller. Mr Miller replied that he was sorry, that nothing in the cross collection could be sold.

Mr Morgan now cried. "Please tell Mr Miller that I will pay anything he wishes, but I must have the cross."

This word he followed with a personal letter to Mr Miller, repeating the wish to have the cross at any price, and enclosing three papal rings, whose settings were exquisite intaglios cut in amethyst and topaz. Sitting before an open fire in his cowled monk's dressing gown of brown burlap, Mr Miller dictated his reply.

My DEAR FRIEND: I cannot find it in my heart to traffic in anything which you value as manifestly you this cross. Take it, with my appreciation of you.

I am returning the three papal rings, which I am sure that you value more than I would know how to do.

Sincerely yours, **FRANK A MILLER**" [258]

Evan in Florida & Pirate Tales

 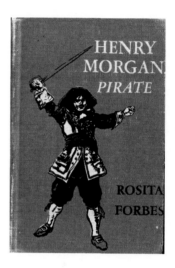

Travel writer Rosita Forbes and her book on Captain
Henry Morgan

In the Spring of 1936, Evan stopped over for a part of the season at Roney Plaza, Florida, USA before darting across by chartered yacht to Jamaica. He stirred the locals of Coral Gables with tall tales about being a "descendant of Blackbeard the pirate who ruled the Old Spanish main 300 years.............. ..[before].." [259] This was a reference in fact to one of the more picturesque of the race ...of Henry Morgan, the buccaneer, who was for a time Deputy

Governor of Jamaica, who died the gallant Sir Henry Morgan. [260] Evan contributed to a book[261] on the pirate by Rosita Forbes.[262]

Mumpumps : Lois' House in Surrey

1933 : Evan's Holy Pilgrimage to Lourdes

In 'The Old Public School Boy's Who's Who' of 1933 [263]Evan listed his 'Recreations' as swimming, aviation, and travel. He also highlighted in his biographical details that he'd once walked in France from Chambery to Lourdes as a part of a holy pilgrimage lasting fifty-six days. This was in the mid 1920s when he acted as a Chamberlain of the Papal Court in Rome, and in fulfilling one of his duties he carried the Papal Blessing to Lourdes, the site of the shrine to St Bernadette.[264]

In earlier volumes of this version of Who's Who to engage the old boys network Evan boasted of being a collector of the works of the Italian Renaissance, but Evan tastes for collecting were varied, and sinister and this included a collection of homoerotic drawings (many by Aubrey Beardsley[265]) and banned works including writings dealing with pederasty and Satanism.

Aldous Huxley, Evan's one time close friend at Oxford in the years of the Great War and who was thought of by Katharine Tredegar as lending a stabilizing influence upon her son, inevitably found fault with Evan about " the swarms of parasitic pederasts, from Egyptian princes to retired sea-captains, who hovered round ... [him] Evan]."[266]

Montparnasse, on the left bank of the Seine in Paris (a meeting place for students and bohemians) was tainted as "ghasdy, a hangout for pederasts." [267] Here, Evan held court alongside his drooling collection of females often dubbed 'fag- hags' the, Nancy Cunard and Nina Hamnett being the leading huskies pulling Evan's sledge, partying till dawn and lapping up sweet compliments and the endless bottles of booze and drugs paid for out of Evan's family purse. Nina had a residence in this Parisian quarter, but Evan fell back on his set of rooms at the Ritz Hotel to sleep though until the roll call for the next session.

It was also at Montparnasse that Evan liked showing off one or other of his latest young male prizes of the bedchamber. But Evan rarely settled for the same companion for very long, he sent a boy packing (but usually well paid) as soon as he caught sight of a pretty new face; Montparnasse provided an entire meat rack of hustlers and impoverished young men from dawn till dawn.

Several of Evan's contemporaries including the writer Cyril Connolly, [268] refer to sightings of Evan in Montparnasse. Evan's invitation of dinner and a swim was difficult to decline by his poorer chums and these often were a precursor to depravity, with local rent boys brought in on tap to fuel the interest and enable Evan to satisfy his particular needs for flagellation and administering punishment.

Evan's Swimming Parties and More Sinister Games

There were several events that shaped Evan's personality and libido; being sexually attacked as a child on Penarth's Pebble beach by a much older male was one indelible memory[269] - but he found solace in the landscape around beaches made of shingle and wild grasses and sand shapes around Brecon (and particularly the dunes on the Island of Bali, where he had his own Beach Hut, and preyed on the primitive local natives); boys, beaches and the sea coast were Evan's constant pull.

Gwyneth (Evan's sister) also suffered a shocking event in her childhood connected with water. Robin Bryans reveals the story:

"When Evan reached his pubescent twelfth and sexually inquisitive year in 1905 and his sister Gwyneth her tenth their parents installed a bathroom at Tredegar [House] ,named later The Cow Bathroom from the collection of [ceramic milk creamers] Staffordshire cows that stood , then as today, on marble shelves behind the shower and bath. The Stewart and Wills children [cousins and friends of cousins from Cardiff and Penarth] went over not just to see the bidet, an unusual feature in British bathrooms, but to experiment with the shower which sprayed water from both sides as well as from above. That started their 'Water Baby Club'.... "[270] during which Gwyneth was 'ducked' by the stronger, older children, until she passed out. Only then was she yanked out of the water. It was a game of dare and double dare, in which Gwyneth always came off worse than the others. Bryans adds "this was a sinister presage perhaps of Gwyneth Morgan's suicide.... by drowning." [271]

Evan always found swimming therapeutic. He routinely bathed alone in the lake in Tredegar Park or for fun and games with house guests. For the more favoured and youthful of the males (with a few local boys invited along too) the main location for covert action was at Sully [a village in Vale of Glamorgan lying on the northern coast of the Bristol Channel] and afterwards Evan provided food and drink by arrangement with a local farmhouse overlooking Lavennock Bay. These encounters spilled over to parties that had no rules or limits. [272]

During the summer months when Evan was abroad he held open air dining, dancing and midnight bathing parties. 'Bring bathing costume' became a standard addition to his social invitations.

The public Lidos of many Europe an cities together with the elegant architectural gems within Parisian and Venetian hotels were Evan's shop window. He adored taking his clothes off. The Piscine Molitor in the 16[th]district of Paris was another favourite stop over by Evan on the prowl ; between the world wars the Molitor was deemed one of the fashionable places to be seen.

The Piscine Molitor: Paris 1929

Evan Succeeds to the Morgan Titles

On 13th February, 1934, Evan left Avonmouth on the steamship Coronado bound for an island romp around Bermuda and the Caribbean. Accompanying him was his twenty-eight-year-old valet, Horace Smith. Master and servant duly transferred to the private yacht of William B Leeds Jnr an American millionaire where the fellow guests included Evan's close friend and sometime lover, Prince Paul of Greece and other members of the international playboy set. [273]

Hon. Evan Morgan Sails Away to Bermuda and returns as Viscount Tredegar

During this trip Evan's father, Courtenay died at the Ritz Hotel, London, on 3rd May, 1934, following his return from a holiday to Australia. It was no little feat tracking Evan down, he eventually returned to Britain, as the second Viscount Tredegar.

Evan the Bachelor Host

A Shooting Party at Tredegar House

"A popular bachelor, whose parties are planned on original lines, is the Hon. Evan Morgan"[274] One peeress remarked thus and added that the parties staged by the bachelor hosts such as Evan were "better planned than those of the average hostess in Society "[275] the perfect ingredients being that the host "takes quite as much pains with the guest list, invites just the right sort of people who will like to meet one another, and the menu usually is an excellent one." [276] Evan's family money ensured this high maintenance life style was supported throughout the 1920s and 1930s. Evan always brought a touch of Bohemia to his parties, with varied guests from all walks of life.

After the death of his father Evan transformed Tredegar House into a showcase for lavish living, with footmen in Regency style outfits and powdered wigs; he traversed the length of the kingdom in order to find handsome male attendants whom he named 'North, South, East and West.'[277]

Evan rises from his sick bed to open an exhibition

Evan refused to let illness affect a promise made to his friend Rupert Mason, a wealthy member of the cotton trade.[278] to open an exhibition at the Alpine Galleries of original illustrations to Mason's book entitled 'The Robes of Thespis.' [279] "The object of the book was to show the varied talent for the designing of theatrical costumes." [280]

Some of Evan's Women and
The Divine Right of Peers

Evan financially supported several ladies with whom he frequently collided socially. Famously, Nancy Cunard (like Lois, another daughter of the rich whose life style was controversial, Nancy had a passionate affair with Henry Crowder, a black American jazz musician.)[281]

In the 1920s Nancy very nearly became a part of the enforced matrimonial plans that Evan was brow-beaten into agreeing to suit his father's standards. The outspoken, high octane living Nancy, daughter of the dazzling London hostess Lady Emerald Cunard, always wished she had taken Lois' place and married Evan (and she would have accepted the same terms made to suit the Society fixers clamouring to save the respective family's reputations of the Morgans and Sturts) .

Evan and Nancy together as one is a most fascinating 'what might have been'. It was said "By any usual definition of love Nancy never loved anyone, including herself..... Living in a largely homosexual literary world she pursued, in drunken sexual rages, male homosexuals, whores, anything, as single-minded as Medea, if not as murderous." [282]In their equally pathetic final fates, Evan and Nancy may certainly have been different, the outcome perhaps explosive but a much better and happier one than the reality.

Other women that Evan loved (but strictly on par as substitutes for losing his sister Gwyneth) included the gin -sodden artist Nina Hamnett. In Wales Evan trusted his dull, conventional cousin Katie Stewart[283] , and to her advantage she knew *everything* about Evan's sexual foibles and illegal trade.

Katie would have made a level-headed Lady Tredegar. The closest any such stability came was when Evan married Princess Olga Dolgoruky[284] in 1939.

Olga had the makings of being a great chatelaine and a successful wife. Alas the odds were stacked against Olga, she truly believed she and Evan would have a normal life together: but he was not able to sleep with her or that matter any woman. Marrying Evan chiefly for money Olga also found out he was broke as well as a great fantasist.

When Evan was flush and purely on a sympathy basis (and as she was a creature, like Evan, a colourful pantomime figure, of deep mood swings and extremes) Morgan money also found its way for their upkeep of the Marchesa Casati, who wanted to be a living work of art. [285]

Evan also made a public stand in his campaign for support for Lord Alfred Douglas, for whom he became a life line in Bosie's sad and crippled old age. This link brought Evan into ensnaring a few other young targets including Richard Rumbold[286] who like Evan was "cagily devoted " [287] to Bosie Douglas.

Evan also contributed to the upkeep of other fellow peers such as Irishman Viscount Valentine Castlerosse [288], a rascal frequently down on his luck who gambled ferociously and was described at his death in 1943 as being " the sort of man of whom it must be said we shall not look upon his like again-with any luck."[289] As some later, no doubt, thought of Evan.

Evan was always surrounded by leeches who connived ways of spending the Morgan money. He was foolish in squandering the allowance from his father on frivolities, and frivolous people in London and during his early years at Christ Church Oxford. From his student days [290] he willingly bailed out this less well-off trusty cousin, Cambridge man Castlerosse, especially as he found him amusing and shared Evan's belief in the divine right of peers over all comers. Evan gained a reputation for displaying a sharp demonic temper, and for hitting out verbally at servants and trades people who wanted to be paid. Of the latter Evan would declare "What more can these people expect? Trades people? Trades people should be honoured by my patronage."

On this Evan also followed exactly the reputation he acquired for being half the spoilt child, half the arrogant adult just as his Irish counterpart Castlerosse.

His biographer Leonald Moseley [291] records of Castlerosse that "He would be moody for hours ... and fly into rages at waiters and maidservants. He would be furious if he didn't get immediate attention, and sweep the soup off the table and scream at the top of his voice. 'Don't stand there, bring me more soup, he would shout, or rush to the telephone and abuse the operator because a number was slow in coming." [292] Such antics as this was also Evan-like behavior at times and these displays of rudeness are supported by comments recorded by Evan's contemporaries from what they witnessed. [293]

In the 1930s Castlerosse became a golf companion to Prince Edward, later the Duke of Windsor. Through this curious attachment he gained a remarkable insight into the private life of the man and woman whom Winston Churchill declared " the greatest love affair of the 20th Century" and Castlerosse's view was that Wallis Simpson had " built up her man" [294] who suffered from " an inferiority complex". [295] Several people cautioned the Duke not to drink too much in Castlerosse's company since he had a tongue for reporting scandal, and he was also a journalist.

Castlerosse was a gossip columnist for Lord Beaverbrook on the Sunday Express newspaper, best known for a column called "Londoner's Log." Evan sided with the stand taken by Beaverbrook's newspapers over the abdication of Edward VIII namely that " the whole issue that ..rocked the British Empire [in 1936] was ..one .. of divorce and it was most unfair, because.. British law permits divorce and remarriage and there is no reason why the law should refer to one Englishman and not to another – there should be no prejudice because what is just for the people also is just for the King." [296] Despite Beaverbrook's defence of Edward, and the Prince's connivance with him to save his throne [297] the Prince despised the news man. [298]

Divine Right of Queers

Evan's Royal links to the Carnegies, the Connaughts and in the company (in Wales and worldwide) with Prince Paul of Greece his regular bedroom comforter overtook closely keeping up with the Windsors. However in the late 1920s and early 1930s Evan did see the Prince of Wales sometimes in the East End of London (supporting Evan's good causes in his back yard as slum landlord in Bromley and Bow and Conservative Parliamentary candidate for Limehouse).

This also spilled over to London functions including the Welsh Guards Club Service Dinners (the Prince of Wales was Colonel of the Regiment)[299], the Derby dances and suppers at Grosvenor House organised by Lady Shelia Milbanke. [300] Evan prided himself in being at the urgent call of all his beloved Princes. At a few theatre first nights and dances in aid of the Prince of Wales' charities Evan was asked to chaperone the Prince's current female favourites and those like Poppy Baring[301] in the inner circle of Prince George, later Duke of Kent. [302] Evan was privy to the Prince of Wales' concerns about George (' PG') (over hard drugs [303] and homosexual relationships [304]).Whilst Edward had also experimented with drugs he suppressed his homosexual tendencies.

PG moved into York House (a wing of St James' Palace) with the Prince of Wales. Outside on the London scene George was mincing about with friends including "cultivated homosexuals" [305] and totals strangers.

Evan knew all the tricks in the book at keeping his gay sex targets from coming back like a boomerang so could offer the Prince of Wales warnings and advice about his brother.

Unlike George (who wrote damning love letters to a young Frenchman [306]), Evan never wrote love letters or kept diaries or notes about his score card. Moreover as Evan and Prince George were equally fond of sleeping with Prince Paul of Greece, Evan was happy to cover up these liaisons; an easy task as Evan, albeit a devotee of 'rough trade' [307] also favoured the privacy of meetings at sea in the company of his own class, on board expensive yachts.

After their youthful larking about, talented male whores were passed between them like the buying and selling of cattle. [308] In 1934, Evan was with Prince Paul on board a New York millionaire's yacht, off Venezuela when the wireless bulletin was heard that Evan was the new Tredegar peer. The year after Evan and Prince Paul repeated a further long, ocean-going cruise together.[309]

The antics of Prince George, Duke of Kent were not halted by his marriage and especially when Princess Marina was pregnant.

One observer is critical " I hear a bad account of PG's conduct during Princess Marina's seclusion. I do wish something could be done about him. Perhaps the baby will make all the difference." [310]

For Evan, one of the consequences of being at close range to Prince George was completely unexpected: Evan fell in love with the blue-eyed, blonde Adonis.

Their relationship was described as an "intense friendship"[311]. Together they frequented a homosexual club in London's Piccadilly called the *Nut House* and got arrested. Release followed as soon as Scotland Yard identified their captives.

One diarist records that " the Kaiser's grandson [Eddie, Baron Ekkehard von Schack] liked Prince George [and it was] said he was artistic and effeminate and used strong perfume." [312] The Baron was almost certainly one of Evan's providers of boys during stays on the Island of Capri. [313]

It was said that the death of Prince George during the Second World War plunged "Evan into despair"[314] and he thought of taking his own life. One witness records "Evan's suicidal mood prevailed long after Prince George's death."[315]

Evan was proud to help the Prince of Wales and especially in the years before Edward gave up his throne.

TREDEGAR HOUSE, TREDEGAR PARK

J. E. THOMAS.

Honeywood House, Rowhook near Dorking

Prince of Wales and Prince George

Evan's delusions meant he got this role out of complete proportion to reality. The Royal requests (at least from the Prince of Wales) were infrequent, but Evan exaggerated his importance to the Royals making up a few stories. An example of this comes from the literary critic Alan Pryce-Jones who relates a laughable tale of Evan conjuring up a summons by Edward, Prince of Wales in order to impress his house guests.

"Evan invited us all to dine at Boulestin's, a restaurant he had lately financed. In the hall, as we left, there lay a note on a tray. He opened it, and blenched, rang a bell, and a footman appeared. "When did this come?" he asked. "An hour ago, sir". Evan turned to us dramatically. "This may have altered the course of history. It's a summons from the Prince of Wales to go at once to York House,. "Well go"... we said... "Too late" he replied, and sternly admonished the footman for not bringing the note at once to his notice.

After dinner, we were asked back for a nightcap. The footman, in indignation, had left the note where it lay and Evan picked it up idly and read it, as though for the first time. "Really, Asprey's are becoming impossible", he said. "They send the bill before they deliver the goods." [316]

Pryce-Jones reflects upon Evan with the precision of a surgeon: " At such moments, his intention was not, I think, to deceive. It was merely that his inventive nature suggested to him a scenario which it was irresistible to act out. Instead of creating the poem or the picture of which he was capable, he used his gift to create an imaginary chapter of life for himself." [317]

Only service to the Pope might take precedence over a command from the Prince of Wales in Evan's madcap name dropping antics. Another ridiculous tale of Evan relates to him running frantically down one of the platforms at Victoria Railway Station in his full Papal uniform shouting out loud (to the amazement of a trainload of cocottes and holidaymakers) that he was carrying important documents...viz " Secret papers for the Holy Father! "[318] and was fully intent on stopping the 'Golden Arrow', the boat train to the Continent that had just left the station.

A Party with Doris Castlerosse

Evan loved to party and in the right company could be witty and clever and could always be relied upon to pay the bar bill. Leonard Moseley records one swell party Evan attended (with wife, Lois) where Doris, Lady Castlerosse [319] was the hostess " At a gay [meaning colourful] table…. Lady Castlerosse was giving a party for Douglas Fairbanks, Lord Carlyle, Lady Oxford, Sir Philip Sassoon, Lady Cunard, Lord and Lady Weymouth, Lord Alington, Mr and Mrs Evan Morgan, Mrs Edwin Montagu, Lord Stanley, Mrs Euan Wallace and Lady Lavery. No bottles of champagne were being drunk, only magnums." [320]

It was a regular Society custom to put on lavish cocktail parties for famous film stars visiting London. In Wales, Evan's neighbour William Randolph Hearst [321] paraded his American celebrities and British luminaries, from Hollywood and London at St Donat's Castle, twenty miles from Cardiff. Through this connection Evan came to know briefly such icons as Charlie Chaplin, Gertrude Lawrence and Fatty Arbuckle. George Bernard Shaw and David Lloyd George were also visitors at St Donats.[322]

Doris Castlerosse   Sir Philip Sassoon

At Doris's party for swashbuckler Douglas Fairbanks, Sir Philip Sassoon [323] was a great art lover, a rich and fussy host (whose mother was from the Jewish banking Rothschild family) and lover of chic. He paraded his wealth and expensive tastes on the Kent countryside and the London scene, entertaining male friends and Prime Ministers. Described as "a very kind creature"[324], but also unflatteringly as having " a bent nose and rather shapeless mouth, filled with prominent teeth [and] not handsome." [325] For many years Philip's name appeared with Evan's as among " Britain's most notable bachelors."[326] In their case this was a euphemism for being queer. [327] Both men engaged Philip Tiden [328], the Society interior designer to make their respective homes "lush and luxurious" [329].

Left: Naps Alington by Ambrose McEvoy
Right: Naps Alington by Augustus John

The "Lord Alington "present at the party was Napier (known as Naps) Sturt, [330] Evan's wife's strikingly good-looking bisexual brother, the 3rd Baron Alington, who had a wild sexual rumpus with Tallulah Bankhead,[331] the American actress and diva. Bankhead pursued Naps like a hound might chase a fox. They ultimately went their separate ways.

One story is of Naps "dining out at a restaurant with his wife when Bankhead came in. As she passed he looked away, but after a few moments, she left her table came over to him and asked in a husky voice: 'What's the matter, darling? Don't you recognise me with my clothes on?'" [332]

Naps' versatile sexual proclivities ranged from sleeping with beautiful women and boys from young to old, including impotent men. He had a serious love affair with Karol Szymanosski, [333] a Polish composer, fifteen years his senior.

Martial Rows of the Castlerosses and the Morgans

Evan's friends, the Castlerosses were well known for their furious marital rows. Surprisingly at the heart of it was not the husband's dalliances but the wife's regular adultery.[334] This was the bizarre reason too for clashes between Evan and Lois. Both Doris and Lois "slept their way through high society." [335]

Evan resented Lois flaunting her bedroom companions in their London home, at 40 South Street, Mayfair, even within hearing distance of his dinner table. This exploded one evening when Evan was hosting a literary frolic for the notable Irish poet William B Yeats. Lois was also hosting her own little gathering of devotees in an adjoining room. Lois overheard Evan castigating her, and burst into Evan's dinner party ordering everyone out of the house. An ugly scene followed between Evan and Lois.[336]   Later, in 1933, the need to exert control and to humiliate Evan (as she tired of his gripes about her lovers – and especially as he had not changed his behaviour in any way) – resulted in an attempt at a show down to plunge their marriage of convenience into chaos. She filed an extraordinary divorce suit (for the era when homosexual conduct was illegal) citing Evan's past acts of sodomy with males in a succession of German hotels. [337]

Before the case reached the newspapers the death of Evan's father Courtenay saved face all round, and 2nd Baron Alington's daughter Lois endured her last days on earth as Viscountess Tredegar, living in her own house of 'Mumpumps' in Surrey, with her horses and dogs and two gentlemen friends. [338] That endurance ended in a bath tub in Budapest in 1937 where Lois was on holiday and getting ready to change for dinner, but suffered a fatal heart attack, aged just 37.

Years of alcohol abuse, slimming pills and starvation to preserve her film star looks and figure were likely underlying causes. The death, although granting Evan greater freedom and some sadness, was not considered suspicious or premeditated or an instance of suicide.

Lois's will, which provoked Evan's secretary to comment "The less said about Lady Tredegar's will the better ..." [339] quickly adding " Lord Tredegar knows nothing about it or its contents" [340] gave the use of her last residence, Mumpumps, Hurst Green, Sussex, to one of her two beloved gentlemen friends. [341]

Hon. Lois Sturt (1900-1937)

LADY TREDEGAR
LEAVES £31,611

Viscountess Tredegar, of Mumpumps, Hurst Green, Sussex, wife of Viscount Tredegar, and daughter of the second Lord Alington, who died, aged 37, at Budapest in September, while on a holiday tour of Europe, left estate of the gross value of £31,611, with net personalty £12,467.

After several bequests she left the use of her residence to Edward George Boulanger and the residue to him for, and remainder to h erniece, the Hon. Mary Anna Sibell Elizabeth Sturt.

342

Evan's Pride in his Kinsmen

David Carnegie

In his more melancholy moments Evan was inspired by the courage shown by several of his kinsmen. One of his heroes was his Uncle David Carnegie[343] the younger brother of his mother, Katharine. An explorer in Australia, David died when Evan was a young boy of seven. The death was usual and tragic (and as the poet Evan saw it, heroic) since David Carnegie was killed " from a poisoned arrow at Koton Kerifi, on the Niger, in West Africa...." where he was working as a mercenary soldier. [344]

Carnegie was from that era of the *Boys Own* gung-ho types expounded by Rudyard Kipling and H Rider Haggard. [345] Evan knew he could never reach such heights. But he listened intently to family stories of David

Carnegie's thirteen month journey across Australia covering nearly 3,000 miles of unmapped and unexplored desert, with four white men and a native tracker. [346]

Godfrey Morgan

Godfrey Morgan

Evan was also proud of his warrior kinsman, Godfrey, 2nd Lord Tredegar, [347] who fought in the battles of the Crimean War:

In Evan's time as custodian of the family's pile, a Boy Scout jamboree was held in the grounds of Tredegar House and Park.

One of the Scouts was charged with the job of getting his patrol across the lake.... Up to his knees in mud, heaving and struggling with logs, ropes and pulleys the boy was later told to " smarten up, straighten [his] woggle, and get on parade, for [he] along with five others had been chosen to be presented to Evan, Lord Tredegar. .." [348]

"We were given tea, shown all the treasures of the house by the great man himself, but of them all, the one that I remember most was the painting in the side hall.

A painting in a gilded frame supported by crossed lances their pennants old and faded, but the painting bold and vivid, of Godfrey, his forebear, then Captain Morgan 17th Lancers, sabre in hand clearing the guns at Balaclava. It made a great impression on a twelve year old, but more so when Evan, Lord Tredegar took down one of the lances, placed it in my hands and assured me that it had been used on the charge. I was mesmerised, and must confess that I am still. " [349]

Some one had blundered!

This short compilation began with a reference to Alfred, Lord Tennyson. It ends with a few lines from the poem of the famous 'Charge of the Light Brigade', which took place exactly 160 years ago today, on 25th October , 1854.

In a curious way these lines are also applicable to Evan Morgan, who even long after his death is still remembered as ' a one-off' character : perhaps

"Some one had blunder'd......"

But:- "They that had fought so well Came thro' the jaws of Death."

William Cross, Newport South Wales
25th October 2014

Evan's Last Affairs

Financial[350]

I

Evan's Death

On 27th April 1949 Evan Frederic Morgan, second Viscount Tredegar, fourth Baron Tredegar of Tredegar Park, Newport, Monmouthshire died aged 55. As Evan had no son, the Viscountcy failed. Evan's uncle, Frederick (Freddie) George Morgan succeeded to the barony as the fifth Baron, and as he died in 1954 he was succeeded by his son John, Evan's cousin. This sixth Baron, John, was born in October of 1908, married in 1954 and died in 1962 leaving a widow and two step daughters but no children of his own blood. Therefore in 1962 the Tredegar line (on the male line) was finally extinct.

At Evan's death in 1949 his uncle Freddie (who now became the fifth Baron) passed everything relating to the Tredegar Estates over to his own son, John (who in 1954 became the sixth Baron – see above). This was to avoid payment of death duties twice within a short period.

New Lord Tredegar renounces his estates

The *Daily Telegraph* of 13th May, 1949 made it clear that the new fifth Baron Tredegar renounced his claim on the Tredegar Estate:

"Lord Tredegar, aged 75 who succeeded a fortnight ago to the barony on the death of his nephew, the second Viscount Tredegar, has renounced the family estates.

Estimated to be worth about £1,150,000, they will go to his son, the Hon. John Morgan, aged 40 who is a bachelor. In his flat over an office in Mount Street, Mayfair, where he lives alone Lord Tredegar told me last night that the transfer was arranged some time before the death of Viscount Tredegar. This was to avoid payment of death duties twice within a short period.

"I am nearly crippled with arthritis, and I have already passed the allotted span of three score years and ten," he said. "I could not cope with all the duties attached to the estates."

It became obvious that some arrangement would have to be made if the estates were be not to swallowed up entirely by death duties levied a second time on his own death. In 1934 their value was £2,300,000, of which about half went in death duties when the first Viscount [Courtenay Morgan, Evan's father] died.

80 per cent payable in duties

"My reading of the position now is that if I had inherited the estates another 80 per cent would go in duties in the event of my own death, leaving very little to carry on the estates. It is difficult to give exact figures. It makes me think that I could sit down and cry when I consider what has got to happen. There will have to be staff cuts and some of our tenants may be displaced if we have to sell farms. None of this need happen if we had not got a government of hungry wolves to whom we are just vermin".

Lord Tredegar said that his son would probably close part of Tredegar House, Newport, Monmouthshire, the family residence, and live in a few rooms. "He is now making a pilgrimage to Lourdes to seek guidance and help in the duties that lie ahead of him."

Property inherited by the second Viscount in 1934 included more than 80,000 acres in Monmouthshire, Glamorgan and Breconshire, Tredegar House, Newport, Honeywood House, Dorking and property in Bow, East London.

A Somerset House official said last night: "When a beneficiary under a will becomes a life tenant of the estate but does not touch it in any way and renounces it as soon as he knows about it, his transfer of the estate to another person is not regarded as a gift liable to duty in the event of his death within five years."

Accumulation of Death Duties

During the lifetime of Evan's father, Courtenay, the third Baron, 1st Viscount (who died on 4th May 1934) there had been difficulties about the payment of surtax arrears and the Inland Revenue were pressing for payment. The nature of the Tredegar Estate was that successive Lords Tredegar had accumulated large death duties but enjoyed a large income from their life interest in the Tredegar Settled Lands but otherwise they had only small capital assets and large tax debts.

At Courtenay's death, family furniture was sold off to the settled land trustees (owned largely by Courtenay) and most of the proceeds of this sale were paid to the Inland Revenue to reduce the tax arrears. But the net effect was that Courtenay still owed over £87,000 arrears, with further years to be assessed. In effect Courtenay's financial affairs were in deep trouble and his estate was hopelessly insolvent.

During the last year of Evan's life the Inland Revenue remitted (i.e. wrote off) large amounts of surtax due from Courtenay's estate. The case was significant enough (in terms of the waiver of large sums of tax, which required explanation in the Board's report) to attract the personal scrutiny of members of the Board of Inland Revenue. Evan's tax papers show that on 1st March 1949 (only a few weeks before he died)   the case was discussed between Board members Sir Eric Bamford, Sir Clifford Wakely and Mr. J H Evans who decided that all but £10,000 of the sums due from Courtenay should be treated as irrecoverable.[351]

Death and Taxes

Evan, Viscount Tredegar dies insolvent

Executors make proposals to Inland Revenue

On 10th May 1949, a few days before the new Lord Tredegar was reported in the Daily Telegraph as renouncing his claims on the family estate,   three   well-dressed, learned gentlemen met together at the headquarters of the British Inland Revenue at Somerset House in the Strand, London WC2.

These wise men were lawyers with duties to discharge from the affairs arising out of the last will and testament of Evan Frederic Morgan, second Viscount Tredegar who had died from cancer a few weeks earlier on 27th April, 1949.

Mr. W B Blatch,[352] Solicitor of Inland Revenue, was the host for the meeting at the request of the two visitors, Mr. James Smith, a Senior Partner of Messrs Rider, Heaton, Meredith & Mills (acting for the Trustees of the Tredegar Settled Estates) and Mr. T. H. E. Edwards[353], the Senior Partner of Messrs Tozers of Teignmouth (acting for the Executors of Evan's will, of whom he was one of the parties representing the interests of Buckfast Abbey).

Quick Calculations

It had already been quickly calculated that at the time of the demise of Evan, Viscount Tredegar, that his own personal estate was completely insolvent as there were large surtax arrears owed by his Lordship to the Inland Revenue.

Edwards made it clear that in the short period of weeks since Evan's death a summary that had been prepared of the deceased's assets and liabilities was believed to be accurate but as there had not been enough time to make a full and complete statement the figures and facts given were submitted as an estimate. Blatch acknowledged this provision.

The estimates declared by the two legal wizards in conjunction with Mr. Blatch suggested that the Executors were rapid and thorough in putting Evan's affairs in order. It was clear that the state of insolvency was "due entirely to the outstanding surtax [now payable] which, all told after all the figures have been ascertained, ... [amounted] to a figure not far below the £200,000."

Besides the tax arrears Evan had other money debts. These included an overdraft at Coutts Bank of £30,000 which was "adequately secured in life assurance policies" and also "domestic, local and trade creditors ... amounting to between £4,000 and £5,000" in Newport, South Wales, and Dorking, Surrey by virtue of his two main family homes at Tredegar House, Newport and Honeywood House, Rowhook, Surrey.

Also payable was the sum of £3,000 owing under a mortgage. Finally Evan was also liable to make two annual payments, one to his past secretary Mrs. Emily 'Mother' Sutherland of £273 per annum and also £250 per annum to his divorced wife, Lady Olga Tredegar. Both these sums were payable as annuities during the lives of the two people involved; Olga's annuity was considered to be "secured on the [Tredegar] settled estates."

Evan's Assets

As to assets, Evan had an interest as "tenant-for-life" of the Tredegar Settled Lands and in the coal compensation payable under The Coal Mines Act 1938. That claim "was yet to be settled and was expected to take time as the Trustees will only pay under the protection of an order of the Court". The record (made after the meeting by Mr. Blatch)   went on to state that the trustees were "at the present marking time pending the result of litigation in similar cases".

The conclusion was quickly reached that whatever Evan's estate was finally fixed at, his entitlement would "fail to be regarded as income in his hands; [moreover] while ... actual cash will amount to several thousand pounds, income tax and surtax may take the major portion."

There was also a claim pending by Evan against the Trustees under the Settled Land Act 1943 which was expected to be a payment to Evan's final estate of several thousand pounds of capital. There was some £12,000 of cash due to Evan on various other accounts and (as tenant-for-life of the Tredegar Settled Lands) he was entitled to an apportioned part of all the rents and other incomes of the settled estates up to the time of his death.

A surplus of £10,000 was due on the life policies (secured to the Bank) after Coutts had repaid Evan's overdraft to themselves. Another life assurance policy taken out for £22,500 was in doubt (given Evan's last illness was a terminal illness) and it was imagined that the sum payable "may be questioned by the life office concerned".

Most of the contents of value at "the family mansions", Tredegar House and Honeywood House, were deemed "heirlooms." It was estimated that the contents of these homes which belonged absolutely to Evan, together with other personal belongings, amounted to something approximating £12,000 in value. Finally there was a reversionary interest under Evan's mother's original Marriage Settlement which was payable to Evan's estate after the death of Katharine, the Dowager Viscountess Tredegar, who at the time of the meeting still survived; she later died in October 1949.

Death Duties

Death duties were not the concern of Messrs Smith and Edwards but it was clear that none would be payable in respect of Evan's own free estate and, as regards the Settled Estates, the Trustees under the settlement were expected to obtain a grant covering this property and they would discharge the duties out of the settled property itself.

The Discussion and Proposals Made to Inland Revenue

The further question to be settled at the meeting was how quickly matters could proceed regarding the administration of Evan's own estate.

Mr. Edwards explained that his co-Executors were the Earl of Southesk, Captain R A Carnegie and the Earl of Carrick. The last named was living in America and was not likely to return for some time.

Edwards went on to explain that he had a proposition supported by Mr. Smith, which was that the Executors would be prepared to prove the late Viscount's will and administer the estate under the general direction of the Inland Revenue provided that three proposals could be agreed.

The three points were that:

First, the Inland Revenue would agree to the domestic, local and trade creditors being paid in full (amounting to £4,000 to £5,000).

Next, the Inland Revenue recognized also that Mr. Edwards' proper fees for acting for the Executors should be paid in full (albeit there was a potential conflict of interest as to the fact that Edwards was himself an Executor).

Lastly, the Inland Revenue would agree to the new Baron (i.e. Evan's uncle Frederick (Freddie) George Morgan, but owing to Freddie's age and infirmity the administration of the Tredegar Estate was expected to passed after due formality of succession to the estate to his son John, Evan's cousin) taking over at a proper valuation the contents of Tredegar House and Honeywood House that did belong absolutely to Evan.

It was stated that Evan's Uncle Freddie and Cousin John Morgan, as well as the Trustees of the Tredegar Settled Lands, did not want a public auction.

Mr. Edwards acknowledged that "the only loss to the [Inland] Revenue in agreeing to these three conditions was that falling under the first condition (payment of the domestic local and trade creditors). It was arguable that the second condition was "no loss as … proper professional charges must be paid."

As far as the third condition was concerned there was no loss arising whatsoever to the Inland Revenue.

Edwards said that the Executors were prepared to act on these conditions because they wished "to preserve the [Morgan] family name position" and spare the estates "from the publicity and scandal that would attend the non-payment of the domestic local and trade creditors and an administration action by the Revenue or any other creditors."

In order to further persuade Mr. Blatch, Edwards outlined that the advantage to the Inland Revenue from accepting these conditions was "not inconsiderable" because such an agreement would "secure that those who are fully acquainted with the [Morgan] family affairs will be in charge of the administration of the estates and this of itself would be a great benefit especially in view of the Coal Act claim, the Settled Land Act claim and the disputed life [assurance] policy".

Blatch raised questions as to the scenario of what might happen if one or other of the Executors refused to act. Edwards' view was that unless a creditor then took out a grant of probate (which it was viewed as being very unlikely other than if it was considered by the Inland Revenue themselves as a way of proceeding), an administration action would be the result and that would be a very costly procedure.

Submission to the Board of Inland Revenue

Blatch submitted Edwards' proposal to the Board of Inland Revenue for approval stating:

"I think that Mr. Edwards can be relied upon to act fairly and prudently in the interests of all and for myself I would recommend the Board to accept the conditions. The matter is one of extreme urgency, however, and I should be glad of the Board's instructions within the next few days for in the meantime the Executors cannot on one hand take any steps in relation to the estate which would be regarded as intermeddling in case they refuse to act and on the other hand they cannot finally refuse to act until the Board has decided on the proposals now made."

The Board of Inland Revenue duly accepted the proposal from Mr. Edwards and the other Executors of Evan's personal Estate.

Edwards and Blatch agreed to have a further meeting on 31st May 1949.

II

31st May 1949

On 31st May 1949 Evan's Executor Mr. Edwards again went to see Mr. Blatch, Solicitor of Inland Revenue, for a further discussion on Evan Morgan's final financial affairs.

At this juncture Edwards was able to provide Blatch with a more accurate picture of the position regarding Evan's assets and debts.

Assets Confirmed

The assets readily realisable were stated as being:

(a) Eight life assurance policies totalling £40,000, subject to a charge in favour of Coutts Bank for nearly £30,000 relating to Evan's overdraft.

(b) A Sun Life policy for £22, 500 free of any charge [No challenge was made by the Assurance Company].

(c) A further Sun Life Policy for £22,000 which was in pursuance of an order of the Divorce Court. This was as part of the security for the annuity of £250 per annum payable to Lady Olga Tredegar for her life.

(d) Cash due to the deceased on various accounts amounting to approximately £12,000 and apportioned income due to him from the Tredegar Settled Estate.

Further assets were confirmed as:-

(a) A reversionary interest under Evan's mother's marriage settlement. Upon this interest there was secured in Scottish legal form a bond for £2,000 at 5% (this is the item previously referred to (incorrectly) as a £3,000 mortgage.

(b) The deceased's personal affects and belongings and his own contents at the family mansions at Tredegar House, Newport and Honeywood House, Rowhook.

(c) The deceased's Settled Land Act claim against the Trustees of the settled lands.

(d) The deceased's claim to compensation under the Coal Mines Act 1938.

(e) The deceased's maintenance claim against the Inland Revenue.

Liabilities Confirmed

The main liabilities of the deceased, other than those mentioned above in relation to the assets on which they are amply secured, were stated as being:

(a) The Inland Revenue for Surtax arrears of over £200,000.

(b) Domestic local and trade creditors (to date) accounting to £2,600. The Executors had already advertised for claims to be sent in and they still expected some claims to follow; the time limit had not yet expired.

(c) An annuity of £273 per annum, unsecured, due to Mrs. Emily Sutherland (Evan's former Secretary) for her remaining life.

(d) Professional fees (mainly accountancy) amounting to approximately £1,000 in relation to the Settled Land Act Claim.

After Edwards was able to clarify the latest position on Evan's estate, he raised various matters with Blatch on which the Board of Inland Revenue's specific instructions were required; on other issues Blatch indicated that the Board was still yet to agree with the course that Edwards had proposed.

These matters are as follows:

(a) <u>The Settled Land Act Claim -</u> Edwards suggested that some attempt should be made to settle this claim against the Trustees. The Trustees and Evan had been at variance on this matter for many years, his claim being for £109,000 which was strongly resisted by the Trustees on the grounds that many of the matters contributing to that sum consisted of expenditure that was covered by maintenance claims which Evan had made. At one time the Trustees had made an offer which Evan refused.

Edwards said he confidently expected to be able to restore amicable relations with the Trustees (on behalf of Evan's Executors) and to re-open negotiations for a compromise deal to be struck. He asked whether in so doing the Executors might accept/ agree a figure without obtaining the Board's instructions.

Blatch was prepared to agree this course of action, especially as:

(i)   Mr. Edwards pointed out that professional fees involved in pursuing the claim had already cost the late Viscount the better part of £2,000 (Evan had paid considerable sums before he died) and as no real progress had been made further heavy costs would result if litigation continued.

(ii) Whatever sum the claim was settled at would, together with the Trustees' Expenses, serve to reduce the value of the Tredegar Settled Estate which was estimated to be worth in the region of £ 2,000,000, consequently duty of 70%, or 75% would be payable. Therefore it would be futile to incur further heavy costs on both sides over a claim which the Inland Revenue was so substantially interested in from both sides.

In his further submission to the Board of Inland Revenue Blatch stated that Edwards (representing Evan's Executors and Smith (the latter representing the Tredegar Settled Estate) could be relied upon to reach a fair settlement.

(b) The 'Schedule A' maintenance claims

Edwards suggested to Blatch that, in the circumstances, it would be a waste of time and expense to strive to agree the 'Schedule A' maintenance claims in every detail since Evan's estate was insolvent and the Revenue's preferential claim might very well exceed all the free assets subject to the agreed debts and expenses.

Accordingly Blatch supported Edwards' attitude to save further expense and said he would asked the Board of Inland Revenue to instruct the Tax Districts concerned to stay negotiations on the claims for the time being.

(c) Lady Olga, Viscountess Tredegar.

Olga, Viscountess Tredegar, Evan's second wife whom he divorced in 1943, was "quite young" (in fact in 1949 she was aged 35 and was born on 13 May 1915).

Edwards suggested that an approach might be made to see whether she would accept a lump sum in settlement of her annuity so that the assets on which this annuity was secured could be released.

The fund involved was valued at £20,000 and was "far more than sufficient to provide for the annuity and some substantial balance can be expected."

Blatch agreed to this suggestion and Edwards confirmed he would report the outcome to Blatch if and when some agreement with Lady Olga had been reached.

(d) The deceased's Mother's Marriage Settlement from 1890.

Evan's mother, Katharine, the Dowager Viscountess Tredegar, was over 80 years of age and not in good health.

Edwards had identified that Evan's interest in his mother's estate (arising from her 1890 Marriage Settlement) could fall into the possession of Evan's Executors in the near future. Edwards proposed to repay the bond of £2,000 secured on Evan's interest in this as soon as possible in order to put an end to the payment of the 5% interest continuing out of Evan's limited assets.

(e) Valuation of furniture, personal effects etc. of the deceased.

It was envisaged that Evan's furniture and personal effects etc would be purchased by the new Lord Tredegar, Freddie, and his son, John.

The Executors had already instructed Mr. John Quilter of Messrs Gooden and Fox of 38, Bury Street, London SW1 to act for them in the valuation.

Mr. Quilter would also act for the Trustees in respect of the valuation of the family heirlooms for the purposes of death duty.

It was suggested a suitable valuer also be appointed by the Board of Inland Revenue and that that appointee and Mr. Quilter should together look over the various articles belonging to the deceased. The valuer appointed by the Board should be well accustomed to valuing antiques of all kinds; Evan's valuable collection of jade was highlighted as one item.

Blatch agreed to ask who the Board of wished to act for them in this matter.

(f) Memorial Service fees and Tombstones

Edwards explained there were fees payable for Evan's two Memorial Services held in London and the one Memorial Service held locally in Newport, South Wales, which amounted to £50.

In view of Evan's position in the British Peerage and other circles, the Executors considered that these fees could not be avoided and ask that the Board of Inland Revenue regard them as a proper part of the funeral expenses. It was also desired to erect a small and simple tombstone on Evan's grave at Buckfast Abbey.

Edwards asked whether the Board would allow this expense - stated to be between £75 and £100 - to be paid.

Edwards was given to understand that the family would otherwise undertake to discharge this expense if the Board could not agree or approve it.

(g) Domestic, local and trade creditors

Edwards explained he would submit a list of the domestic local and trade creditors to the Board of Inland Revenue before he settled any of the various accounts. He announced that he had already discharged a few of the small items, i.e. the weekly wages of manual employees who could not be kept waiting and who might also claim to be preferential.

See APPENDIX 1 for the full list of those creditors and trades people ultimately paid.

(h) <u>Professional fees</u>

The professional fees payable arose out of the Settled Land Act claim.

Blatch acknowledged that these "must be accepted that they be paid as a proper charge against the proceeds of the claim."

Edwards made it known that he would like to have the Board of Inland Revenue's permission to discharge these accounts.

(i) <u>Mrs. Emily Sutherland's Annuity</u>

Edwards advised Blatch that the annuity in respect of Mrs. Emily Sutherland (Evan's former Secretary) was unsecured and consequently, unless the final Estate was sufficient to provide the Inland Revenue with more than enough funds to meet its preferential claim, Mrs. Sutherland would receive nothing.

In reply to Blatch's question about whether Mrs. Sutherland was aware of the position Edwards confirmed that she was fully aware of the situation and so far has not made any claim.

(j) <u>Equipment in Evan's Private Chapel at Honeywood House</u>

Details emerged that showed that Evan maintained a private chapel at Honeywood House which contained such things as a gold chalice, vestments and other articles which had been blessed by the Roman Catholic Church and that the items were actually used in the church services.

Edwards informed Blatch that it was his understanding that under canon law these items could not be sold off. It was the wish of Evan's family that they "take over these articles and will continue to upkeep the chapel and its contents but in the circumstances do not wish to pay the market price for the gold chalice, to take an example."

Edwards suggested that some fair value might be fixed which was satisfactory to the family and the Inland Revenue.

Blatch agreed to submit this question to the Board of Inland Revenue for instructions.

The other contents of the chapel such as candlesticks etc. had not been blessed and there was no bar on the sale of these under canon law.

Edwards suggested that the family purchased these at market price.

(k) Consumable stores at Honeywood House

Edwards said it was proposed to assess the items of 'Consumable stores' at Honeywood House as at the date of Evan's death in the sum of £200.

In reply to Blatch asking about a physical check on these stores Edwards said he had made a cursory examination and was satisfied that that was a fair price Edwards added that there was no large stock of wines or spirits.

(l) The deceased's covenants

Except for the covenants in favour of Mrs. Emily Sutherland and Lady Olga, Viscountess Tredegar, all the covenants of the deceased terminated with his death so far as Edwards could ascertain.

There might be small apportioned sums due under these covenants, many of which were in favour of old Morgan employees and other poor personae.

Edwards mentioned that he might ask the Board of Inland Revenue to allow these small sums to be paid out in the same way as the domestic, local and trade creditors but he would first ascertain what sums were involved and submit a list later if the Executors decide to make any request to the Board of Inland Revenue.

Blatch thanked Edwards for all the work he had done on Evan's affairs.

In this submission to the Board of Inland Revenue Blatch recorded:

"I should like to add that I am most impressed with Mr. Edwards' handling of this matter."

Blatch also had oversight of Evan's surtax papers. These papers indicate that Blatch returned the file to the Special Commissioners as it was considered that it would be some considerable time before it was necessary to decide the exact amounts of the Inland Revenue's total claims and what were deemed to be its preferential claim.

Edwards agreed to have a further meeting with Blatch on 10th August 1949.

III

10th August 1949

On 10th August 1949 Mr. Edwards called again on Mr. Blatch, Solicitor of the Inland Revenue, at Somerset House for a further discussion on Evan Morgan's last affairs.

Before listing the matters that were to be discussed Blatch said that he wished first to record that Messrs Sotheby and Co had agreed to act for the Inland Revenue in the valuation of the Morgan furniture etc.

The cost were discussed. At Honeywood House the special fee of 1% on the first £10,000 and 10/- (ten shillings) above that figure plus travelling expenses.

Blatch announced that the valuation has now been made and a certified copy has been received at Somerset House giving a figure of £8,837.15s.0d agreed by the two valuation companies involved, Messrs Gooden and Fox Ltd. and Messrs Sotheby and Co. The Valuers had been asked to send a note of their charges.

The following matters were raised and discussed between Blatch and Edwards:-

(a) The valuation of furniture etc. at Honeywood House

Mr. Edwards referred to the Sotheby/ Fox valuation and reported that John Morgan had already sent him a cheque for £8,837.15s.0d (the amount of the valuation) and had been allowed to purchase the furniture etc. from Honeywood House. Mr. Edwards had mentioned this to Blatch's colleague, Mr. Weston, earlier by telephone and had agreed, following the Board of Inland Revenue's order of 11ᵗʰ May 1949, that there was no objection to this course so far as the Board was concerned. The hurry was due to the desire to empty Honeywood House as soon as possible to cut down the expenses.

(b) The consecrated articles in the Private Chapel

Mr. Edwards reported that it was now understood that the articles relating to Evan's Private Chapel, which were not included in Sotheby/ Fox valuation referred to above, did not amount to more than £100. In the circumstances, and bearing in mind the difficulty in saying definitely what had and what had not been consecrated, it was proposed to obtain a certified valuation from Mr. John Quilter of Messrs Gooden & Fox and John Morgan would pay that amount to the Executors as the purchase price so that consequently no further questions might arise in this matter.

(c) Mr. John Quilter's fees for the valuation

Blatch suggested that whilst the valuer, Mr. Quilter, had been engaged by Evan's Executors, John Morgan was obtaining the benefit of his valuation. Accordingly Blatch argued that John Morgan might feel disposed to at least pay a proportion of Mr. Quilter's fees. Edwards agreed to raise this matter with John Morgan.

(d) The late Viscount's personal effects at Tredegar Park, Newport.

It was understood by Edwards that the furniture etc. in all the main rooms were heirlooms i.e. part of the Settled Estates in which the late Viscount had only a life interest and that his own personal effects were limited to the contents of the kitchen, servants' rooms and other minor rooms. It was estimated that the value of these contents was no more than £500 but the question was whether the Board of Inland Revenue wished an independent valuation to be made or would they be satisfied to accept Mr. Quilter's figure. Edwards confirmed that John Morgan would purchase these contents in any event at the agreed figure.

There was some doubt, in fact, as to whether some of the contents of the minor rooms might not also be heirlooms but Edwards thought that the Executors would be advised not to press strongly for a detailed list of what were heirlooms and what were not but to accept the line of demarcation that the main rooms contained the heirlooms while the minor rooms did not. Blatch accepted that Edwards and Quilter were best able to advise on the matter and Blatch recommended to the Board of Inland Revenue that Quilter's figure of valuation be accepted without requiring any independent valuation. The type of articles involved would in any event not justify Messrs Sotheby and Co. going to visit Tredegar Park.

(e) Exception on Grounds of historic interest

In view of the insolvency of Evan's estate, Edwards told Blatch he would not go to the trouble of claiming exemption from estate duty under section 15 (2) of the Finance Act 1894. This was in respect of such items at Honeywood House (of historic interest) belonging absolutely Evan which may have been regarded as a claim to fall within this section.

(f) Articles in Ireland

It emerged that Evan had taken a rental on a furnished house in Ireland and had found it necessary to supplement the furniture by certain other equipment. These items would be valued when the Executors received details in

England. Edwards predicted that John Morgan would take these assets over at their respective valuation; it was in any case a small item of some £50 at the most and Blatch agreed that the Board would not require an independent valuation.

(g) Messrs Stephenson, Harwood and Tatham, Solicitors.

Edwards advised that the law firm of Messrs Stephenson, Harwood and Tatham[354] had previously acted for Evan during his lifetime and they held a general power of attorney. At intervals money was paid to this firm generally on account of work done or to be done. At the time of Evan's death the firm advised that this figure included the professional fees in respect of Evan's claims against the Trustees of the Tredegar Settled Lands and payments made by this firm of £160 to other professional firms. Edwards did not think this bill would be in any way attacked as excessive and thought (as did Blatch) that the firm had a lien [355] on the sum of £500 held by them. In the circumstances Blatch and Edwards agreed that the Executors had no option but to accept that Messrs Stephenson, Harwood and Tatham were entitled to retain the sum of £375 approximately but could be called upon only to pay over the balance of £125.4s.8d.

(h) Mrs. Sutherland's Annuity

Edwards informed Blatch that the annuity to Evan's former secretary, Emily Sutherland, was for the sum of £273 net and that Mrs. Sutherland had recently enquired as to her position. Sutherland was said to be a lady aged approximately 50 years old and the annuity was paid "after many years of faithful service rendered to the Viscount".

However, this annuity was not supported by any funds. Edwards pointed out that if Evan's estate was sufficient to pay more than the Inland Revenue's preferential claim, Mrs. Sutherland would be prejudiced by the agreement between the Inland Revenue and the Executors that they should be permitted to pay in full the domestic, local and trade creditors unless the Board of Inland Revenue agreed that, on the division of the estate, Mrs. Sutherland must be paid the sum due to her upon the basis of strict administration.

Blatch considered the position was that other creditors must be paid their due share on a strict administration. It was implicit in the Board of Inland Revenue' s agreement (from the Executor's angle) that it was essential that they must be protected from any complaint that they were favouring one creditor over another.

Blatch said he would make a suggestion to the Board of Inland Revenue that would, in effect, mean that the sum available after meeting preferential claims was divided into the amount of the non-preferential claims to ascertain the non-preferential dividend. Mrs. Sutherland would receive her proper share/dividend with the Inland Revenue bearing the cost of certain non-preferential creditors being paid in full.

Edwards said he was not concerned to press the point that Mrs. Sutherland should be given more than her proper share/dividend but he was concerned to protect the Executors and make sure there was no misunderstanding. It was envisaged that Mrs. Sutherland would accept a compromise sum in full and final settlement but that need not be explored yet or even at all if the administration could be completed without undue delay or complications.

(i) Katharine, the Dowager Viscountess Tredegar's Marriage Settlement

The value of the investment held under Evan's mother's Marriage Settlement was £13,700 and these investments stood irrevocably appointed to the late Viscount on the death of his mother, Katharine, who was now aged 84. Edwards reminded Blatch that there was a bond in Scottish form of £2,000 secured on Evan's reversionary interest but this asset (disposable upon Katharine's death) was a larger one than it was at one time anticipated to be.

(j) Lady Olga Tredegar, Evan's Second Wife (divorced)

Edwards had established that Olga owed Evan, her former husband, the sum of £534. Olga's ability to pay this sum or any part of it was doubted but it was thought by Evan's Executors that this debt might be a useful lever in order to obtain Olga's agreement to the proposition that she should be paid a lump sum in full and final settlement of her annuity.

Blatch viewed that a compromise agreement with Olga was all the more desirable now by reason of the fact that her £250 (gross) annuity per annum was returned/ funded by Evan's life interest in the Tredegar Settled Lands as well as on a life assurance policy for £20,000 and his reversionary interest in his mother's Marriage Settlement.

Accordingly Edwards informed Blatch that the Trustees of the Tredegar Settled Lands had given notice regarding the "Olga" annuity settlement, which Edwards thought they were entitled to do. The effect of this move was that any accrued income due but not paid over to Evan already should be paid to them instead of the Executors. The sum involved would amount to thousands, rather than hundreds, of pounds and there would also be interest due and the aggregate amount would swell the capital that was already far more than sufficient to produce the return to pay Olga's annuity.

Edwards understood that any surplus income would be paid to the Executors until Lady Olga died. Blatch thought that such a protracted administration was not desirable and he agreed that the time was ripe to suggest tentatively that possibly Lady Olga's annuity rights could be surrendered by her for a one-off capital sum. Subsequently, the sum of £5367.14s 2d (based on figures for purchase of a like annuity) was offered to Olga, via Tozers. The debt due to Evan's Executors of £534 was "kept in abeyance for bargaining purposes". A counter-proposal was subsequently received for £6000 plus the release of her debt.

(k) Debt of 1,000 Swiss francs incurred by Evan in Italy.

Edwards advised that the Executors had received a claim for a relatively small sum in respect of an amount owed by Evan as a result of a transaction which infringed the currency regulations. The cost has arisen after Evan fell ill in Italy and he needed the extra money and it was for this purpose that a friend in Italy had helped him out with a loan.

Blatch agreed that this was a valid claim.

(l) Evan's Debts in England

Edwards said that in response to Press advertisements the total claims notified so far (and the period has not quite expired) amounted to £4,800. In addition there would be the item of the apportioned sums due under Deeds of Covenant that expired on Evan's death. This figure quoted included an item of over £800 in respect of accountancy fees due to Messrs Peat, Marwick, Mitchell & Co. in respect of maintenance claims, the Settled Land Act claims and possibly other work where details were awaited. The Executors were not necessarily contending that this item fell within the protected agreement for "domestic, local and trade creditors". A full list of Evan's debts would be submitted to the Board of Inland Revenue in due course for the Board's agreement as to what are considered to fall within that phase " domestic, local and trade creditors" .

(m) <u>Telephones at Honeywood House</u>

The Executors wanted also to advise Blatch that there were sums due on the telephones at Honeywood House which had been of great use both to the Executors and the Morgan family since Evan's death. Edwards proposed that he should agree with John Morgan a fair apportionment of the fairly heavy telephone bills for the period since the deceased's death. Blatch agreed that this course was desirable.

(o) <u>Memorial Services and Tombstones</u>

Blatch advised Edwards that the Board of Inland Revenue would not object to the cost of Evan's memorial services (a point raised at an earlier meeting). This cost could be included as part of the funeral expenses but it was not considered appropriate to allow the cost to the Executors for the erection of any tombstones as this might cause difficulty in view of the death duty practice of excluding such cost. Edwards said that he would not press this small matter so that it no longer needed to be considered further.

(p) Settled Land Act 1943 Claim: Compromise with the Tredegar Trustees

One other important matter from an earlier meeting was that Edwards sought agreement from the Board of Inland Revenue to reach a compromise to the outstanding   claim against the Trustees of the Tredegar Settled Land at Evan's death under the Settled Land Act, 1943. This solution was suggested to save heavy costs on both sides and Blatch had previously concurred but a problem had arisen between the Executors and the Trustees.

Edwards stated that the Trustees of the Tredegar Settled Land were doubtful whether they had the power to compromise insofar as the matter was one for the discretion of a Judge. Blatch noted that Edwards (and his fellow Executors) considered that if the proposal of a compromise was backed by the opinion of learned Counsel and that Trustees were fully protected then the matter could proceed. The Executors were going to explore further this possibility with Mr. James Smith, the lawyer from Messrs Rider, Heaton, Meredith and Mills who had attended the first meeting with Blatch and who acted for the Trustees of the Tredegar Settled Lands. A further suggestion from Edwards was that it would in any event be worthwhile obtaining Counsel's opinion on this point at issue. Blatch agreed. The plan was for Mr. Smith to be approached to see whether a case could be put up to a junior Counsel of standing for his opinion at joint expense.

(q) The schedule of Evan's Maintenance Claims

Blatch informed Edwards that it would be necessary to work out these maintenance claims, if only for the purpose of enabling John Morgan, the new tenant for life, to use his predecessor's average.

It was also stated by Blatch that the sum involved was not expected to be more than £1,000 in tax and that perhaps matters could be settled more quickly on a fair basis if there was give and take on both sides. Edwards was anxious not to incur further heavy professional fees and hoped that he would not have to instruct Messrs Peat, Marwick, Mitchell and Co. any further. There was a meeting planned between Edwards and John Morgan and the Estate Agent and Edwards would see what could be done towards a speedy and fair settlement. Blatch said that if the Board agreed, the Tax Inspector involved at District level could be told that provided those acting on the other side are co-operative and prepared to act on a give and take basis, then he might request that the Tax Inspector also act on that basis in order to arrive at a fair and speedy settlement.

(r) The Inland Revenue Affidavit.

The Executors were shortly to apply for Probate on Evan's Estate.

Blatch's observation (albeit he appreciated everything that Edwards had done to date) was that from the information contained in the present Revenue affidavit it was a fact that the majority of the items, both credit and debit, were not capable of being calculated with much exactness and had therefore been included on an estimated basis. Insofar as it was apparent that the estate was insolvent, Edwards said he was anxious that the Estate Duty Office should at least delay raising their usual enquiries until there had been time to work out more accurately the extent of the overall deficiency. Blatch endorsed his file that Edwards had asked this only because he was already working in close touch, through the Inland Revenue Solicitor's Office, with The Board of Inland Revenue.

Blatch submitted a long report to the Board of Inland Revenue setting out all the facts and factors to be recorded on the papers for future reference. The only matters on which the Board's instructions were needed quickly were, firstly, whether the Board was satisfied to rely on Mr. Quilter's valuation. Secondly, Blatch also requested the Board's agreement to his conclusion on the question raised under Mrs. Sutherland's claim to annuity and reaching a one-off settlement figure. Finally he asked the Board to, in due time, instruct the Inspector of Taxes at Newport (Monmouthshire) regarding the Estate Duty Office on the respective points previously raised.

Before this report was typed Blatch received instructions verbally (after consultation with the Board) on matters discussed with Edwards on the valuation of the items in Evan's Private Chapel and regarding Evan's other effects.

IV

Income Tax Year ended 5th April 1950

Probate of the Will of the late Viscount was granted to his Executors on 29th December 1949. [356]

In Blatch's report to the Board of Inland Revenue as at 5th April 1950 he advised that Evan's Executors held in hand ample funds to pay off Evan's debts other than the income tax and surtax amounts payable.

Mr. Edwards of Messrs Tozers now requested permission from the Board of Inland Revenue to pay the debts that fell within the description of "domestic, local and trade creditors".

Blatch also noted from the meeting with Edwards in May 1949 that there were also the funeral expenses and certain testamentary expenses incurred.

Blatch summarised the position to the Board regarding the payment of the "domestic local and trade creditors" in full as being one of the conditions upon which the Executors agreed to act and at the outset this was estimated at being between £4,000 and £5,000.

A list of what are referred to as Ordinary Debts which formed part of the Inland Revenue Affidavit was submitted by Blatch to the Board. Blatch requested confirmation that he could proceed to authorise the payment of all those debts. The exceptions (which were highlighted in Blatch's report) comprised the Revenue debts, the bank overdraft to Messrs Coutts that had been discharged out of the life assurance policies on which it was secured and the debt to Messrs Peat, Marwick, Mitchell & Co. of £895. With the exclusion of these items a total of £5,265.16s.11d. was due and consisted of the proportionate sums under various deeds of covenant up to the date of Evan's death.

Blatch considered that a few of the debts included in this total of £5,265.16s.11d. merited some further remarks.

The deceased's Covenants

Evan's various "covenants" have been previously referred to in Chapter II and relate to sundry items and pensions to former Estate staff. Mr. Edwards, representing Evan's Executors, advised Blatch that he was not claiming that these sums due all fell within the description "domestic local and trade creditors". There was however an amount standing at £522.19s.11d which represented sums due under covenants for pensions to old employees etc. In his submission Blatch believed that the Board may wish these to be paid in full. As regards a further covenant involving the payment of £431.7s.10d, Blatch asked Mr. Edwards to make sure that the payments covenanted were made more apportionable.

Norman Brett Ltd. – Bookmakers

Edwards pointed out that the sums owed to Norman Brett Ltd was a sum due to a firm of bookmakers. In the circumstances this was considered a debt of honour. The Executors would settle the claim.

Sums due to Messrs Reddick and Tyler

Edwards checked the claims for Messrs Reddick and Tyler as closely as possible. While the paperwork was not entirely satisfactory, Edwards accepted that the sums were due and the Executors also wished to discharge the debt.

Blatch submitted the list of all items deemed "domestic, local and trade creditors". He asked the Board of Inland Revenue to indicate whether it was agreed that all of the debts totalling £5,265.16s. 6d. may be paid in full or, if not, to what extent they may be paid in full. The figure of £5,265.16s.6d had been worked out by Blatch on the basis that the pencilled totals on the list were accurate. A provision was made that some slight adjustments may be necessary as regards the proportions of pensions and annuities payable under the Deeds of Covenant.

Monies Owed Outside of Great Britain

Blatch also submitted to the Board of Inland Revenue for clearance a list of debts due to persons outside Great Britain. One debt due to Decostier was regarded as "suspicious" by Edwards, otherwise the Executors were satisfied that the sums involved were due and payable. Blatch asked the Board of Inland Revenue to agree to leave the payment of these debts in full to Edwards' discretion. Edwards was also to obtain such consents as were necessary from Exchange Control in view of any currency or exchange regulations applicable.

Dr Sandoz

As regards Dr. Sandoz (this debt was the one referred to in Chapter III) Blatch commented that it was his view that the Board would not wish to stand in the way of payment of this claim, but beyond that the Board had no interest. Blatch cautioned that the Executors must act at their peril if, in honouring this debt, any penalty was incurred.

Edwards also asked Blatch whether the Executors could proceed to pay Evan's funeral expenses of £106.15s.0d. and the cost of his three memorial services, totalling £26.18s.0d. There were also associated costs for newspaper announcements of Evan's death and notice of the Memorial Services totalling £15.6s.0d. Similar requests were made for payment of the valuation fee and the expenses of Messrs Gooden & Fox totaling £151.12s. 2d.

There was also an outstanding claim from Lord Southesk for his travelling expenses of £25 (he was one of the Executors and lived at Kinnaird Castle in Angus, Scotland) and finally there were charges and disbursements by Messrs Tozers' (Edwards' firm) amounts up to the date of probate amounted to £572.8s.6d. Blatch recorded that he was examining the Tozers' detailed bill of costs but did not expect to be able to criticize it in any way; however, subject to this proviso these costs had to be paid in full as a part of the testamentary expenses as also the other expenses mentioned above. The Board agreed to the cost of the memorial services being regarded as part of the funeral expenses – see Chapter II.

Blatch asked the Board to signify their agreement to the payment of all these costs and also, to avoid troubling the Board unnecessarily, to provide him with authority to agree on their behalf to the Executors paying any further administrative costs that necessarily had been or fell to be incurred.

The debt of £895 to Messrs Peat, Marwick, Mitchell & Co.

Edwards announced that he was looking into the debt involving Messrs Peat, Marwick, Mitchell & Co. very closely. This represented professional fees in relation to work connected with Evan's surtax arrears and other tax affairs. It was thought probable that the account would have to be paid in full, not only because parts of the amount were the costs in respect of the Tredegar Settled Land Act claim but also to secure the continued assistance of this firm; it might also be that the firm could claim something further in the nature of a lien in respect of papers and records they had prepared. Edwards said he would endeavour to settle this debt as best he could and asked whether the Board would allow the matter to proceed on that basis, i.e. to give Edwards authority to settle the debt on the best terms available.

Count Daschkow

Count Daschkow was the brother of Olga, Viscountess Tredegar. Evan had place £500 on deposit with solicitors Messrs Stephenson Harwood & Tatham "as a backing for Count Daschkow having been allowed to enter the USA on a date ... prior to the 1939/45 war". The transaction had been conducted by Evan's legal wizard Mr. Oppenheimer who was dead at the time that Evan's executors were rounding up everything by way of assets in Evan's estate. Oppenheimer's offices had also been destroyed by bombing during the Second World War.

Subsequently the Foreign Office was approached by the Inland Revenue who in turn asked the Consular Section of the British Embassy in Washington to make some further enquiries. The British Embassy contacted the US Department of Justice (responsible for Immigration and Naturalisation Services) in August 1949. At first nothing was found in the USA relating to Daschkow. Solicitors Stephenson Harwood & Tatham's position was that "unless a more definite reply [could] be obtained from the USA Authority they would not part with the £500 except in return for a suitable indemnity."

An address for Daschkow was found in New York in 1941 (135 East 79th Street, New York 21) and a further effort was made to trace the USA authorities to follow things up. This produced a further response from the US Immigration and Naturalisation Bureau to the effect that there was no indication that an immigration bond was required by Daschkow. This allowed Blatch to give Stephenson Harwood & Tatham the necessary indemnity they required to release the £500.

I should be glad to know whether the Foreign Office has received any further information concerning this matter since I passed on details as to the whereabouts of this individual at the end of October last.

Settlement with Mrs. Emily Sutherland

Blatch thought that to entitle Mrs. Sutherland to receive £6,000 would mean that the overall deficiency would have to be reduced to about £50,000, i.e. that the Settled Land Act must produce £56,000 more than the £30,000 so far included, but he conceded that his calculations were subject to correction.

Blatch records: "I should be glad to know whether the Board wishes in any way to amend its previous instructions in the matter e.g. by reducing the ceiling of the amount it is prepared to agree to a reduced figure from £6000 to say £5,000. I think such a course would be justifiable in view of the new developments. The matter is of some urgency as negotiations should I think commence before the expiry of a year from the death, i.e. before 27th April next."

V

Tying Up Some Loose Ends

The last affairs of Evan, Viscount Tredegar rumbled on for several more years.

Mrs. Emily Sutherland

On 18th April 1950 Mr. W B Blatch, Solicitor of Inland Revenue, wrote to a colleague in Taxes Division named R C Nicholas to confirm that he had been advised that Emily Sutherland (Evan's former Secretary) was prepared to accept £5,000 in settlement of all her claims under the Deed of Covenant dated 12th May 1943 and an Annuity Deed dated 24th April 1943 which came to an end with Evan's death. A further report from Blatch dated 23rd May 1950 explained that matters were about to be settled, fully and finally, with Emily Sutherland over her annuity claim.

"The Deed of Release has been drawn in such a way that (a) in consideration of £5,000 Mrs. Sutherland releases the deceased's Executors and his estate from the annuity which did not cease with the deceased's death and all claims in respect thereof and (b) Mrs. Sutherland admits that she has received all payments due in respect of both annuities up to 1st April 1949 and releases the Executors and the deceased's estate from any further liability. While it would appear that on the basis of this Deed there can be little prospect of establishing that any part of the £5,000 is an income payment, I have given the assurance on behalf of the Board that no claim for income tax will be made against Mrs. Sutherland. The Executors, with my approval, have agreed to pay Mrs. Sutherland's solicitors' charges of £16.16s 0d."[357]

The late Katharine, Dowager Viscountess Tredegar

Another loose end was sorted at the same time relating to Evan's mother, Katharine, and the transfer to Evan's final estate of the proceeds of the Carnegie family Marriage Settlement.

Blatch confirmed to the Board of Inland Revenue:

"The estate of the late Viscount Tredegar became entitled on the death of his mother to the funds of the Marriage Settlement. Messrs Tozers informed me that there would be a delay in handing over these funds because various death duty points of difficulty had to be settled. After getting provisional approval to my suggestion, and subject to the Board's concurrence, I suggested as a means of avoiding both delay and expense that the Trustees of the Settlement should, with the authority of the Executors of the late Viscount's Will, hand over the whole of the funds in their hands on the understanding that if and when the duty payable on the death of the late Katharine Tredegar in respect of these funds is formally assessed no duty would be collectible from them (an assurance to this effect being given to the Trustees by the Revenue) and that the responsibility for contesting any formal assessment should fall on the Executors".

This suggestion was approved by the Executors and the Trustees and, upon the approval of the Board of Inland Revenue, Blatch gave the necessary assurance to all parties and obtained the funds of the Marriage Settlement for allocation.

Blatch also concluded that following the ascertainment of Evan's exact surtax liability there was much less likelihood than ever of the Viscount's estate showing a surplus. Accordingly it was not considered necessary to arrive at the exact death duty liability in respect of the Marriage Settlement funds unless the issue was a straight-forward matter.

The Trustees of the Marriage Settlement arranged to pay the proportion due on the income from that Settlement to bring that particular matter to an end.

Coal Compensation Money

Blatch continued to work heroically rounding up other sums from Evan's estate. He reported that £30,000 had been received from various sources.

He also explored additional income that Evan may have received (not referred to by the Executors) potentially raising the extent of the overall surtax arrears.

"I received information which led me to suppose that the late Viscount had received substantial payment of income derived from the Coal Compensation Monies which would not have been included in the surtax debt and was probably a little on the low side "

The Executors had sent in returns but Blatch remained unconvinced:

"Surtax returns have now been rendered for all years and it is possible to say now that the surtax liability outstanding at the date of death for all years is about £246,750."

This was viewed as "a firm figure agreed by Special Commissioners subject to minor queries, based on full returns and taking into account all subsidiary matters such as maintenance claims, excess rents etc."

To safeguard the Inland Revenue Blatch made a provision that there could be "further surtax liability which will result ... in respect of the claim on the capital of the Coal Compensation Monies."

<u>Evan's Personal Allowances, Deductions and Revised Deficiency</u>

Blatch submitted figures to the Board of Inland Revenue, taking into account the sum of £1,000 which was due to Evan in respect of his personal tax allowances up to the date of death and also taking into account the maintenance claims, Schedule D Excess Rents assessments and the 'Schedule A' arrears, which together resulted in a net repayment due of £1,205.7s.9d. as against an estimated liability of £3,500 which increased the surtax debt.

A revised figure of the probable deficiency between the proceeds from Evan's personal estate and taxes due was around £106,000.

Settled Land Claim

Blatch was mindful that one factor that might reduce the deficiency to any material extent (apart from the death of John Morgan without male issue) was dependent on the successful outcome of the Settled Land Act Claim.

An estimate of a return of £30,000 was made by Blatch although he admitted that a bigger sum might result. Blatch's colleague, a Mr. Stamp, had been consulted by Evan's Executors regarding deductions.

Blatch was cynical: "Whilst [Mr. Stamp] does not support any extravagant views concerning the claim, he does not regard the excessive living expenses and [unresolved issues around] deeds of covenants as being necessarily too harmful provided that the actual expenditure on the Tredegar properties did exceed the available income after allowing for taxation paid or payable."

The remaining issue was the Revenue's preferential claim on Evan's estate (with almost all other creditors being non-preferential). The estimated deficiency of £106,000 was deemed to be borne between the preferential Revenue claim of £183,450 and the remaining non-preferential creditors of £13,000.

VI

12ᵗʰ November 1952

On 12ᵗʰ November 1952 a further report on Evan's last affairs was submitted to Taxes Division by the Solicitor of Inland Revenue. Mr. Blatch had by now retired and his successor, Mr. R B Waterer,[358] was able to summarise the state of play regarding the administration of the estate.

Payments to Inland Revenue

Payments were confirmed as held on account of the arrears of surtax amounting to £40,000, £30,000, £15,000, £11,928.4s.11d., £6,000 and £14,000, a total of £116,928.4s.11d.

The amount of £11,928.4s.11d. was the sum received in November 1950 from Katharine's Marriage Settlement, being funds that fell into Evan's estate following the death of his mother. Something over £3,000 of the sum was attributable to death duty.[359]

The Coal / Mineral Compensation Claim

The coal and mineral compensation claim came before the Courts in May 1952. The late Viscount's estate was held to be entitled to receive £25,568. After deduction of tax at 9/6d in the £ under Rule 21, i.e. £12,144.16s.0d., there remained a net sum of £13,423.4s.0d which had been paid over to the Executors by the Trustees of the Tredegar Settled Estates. Subject to the taxation and payment of costs, ordered to be paid by the Trustees, that claim had now been disposed of.

Settled Land Claim from the Tredegar Settled Land Trustees

Evan's Executors were still pursuing the Settled Land Act claim from the Trustees of the Tredegar Settled Land Estates and there were still a few matters to settle with them. The Trustees had, despite much pressure, still not paid over the full sum due to the estate in respect of the apportioned rents and other income up to Evan's death. It is not known why there was an ongoing difficulty on this matter. As Evan died on 27th April 1949 the figures should have been made available. Substantial payments (£20,000 in all) on account had however been received and Messrs Tozers (on behalf of Evan's Executors) were pressing for an account and payment of the balance that was due.

Minor Disputes

There were also a few minor disputes which it was hoped to settle. These were:

(a) A debt due to Evan's Executors by John Morgan in respect of live and dead stock taken over by him (£548.17s.9d.).

(b) A claim by John Morgan that some articles purchased by him from the Executors (£481.10s.0d. was paid for them) were in fact heirlooms.

(c) A claim by the trustees of the Settled Estate against the Executors in respect of missing heirlooms and damage done by the deceased to heirlooms.

It was expected that these matters would be settled by setting (b) and (c) against (a). There was no dispute as to (a) and it seems clear that the claim under (b) could be substantiated. As to (c) it appears that Evan may well have caused damage to heirlooms and as receipts were produced showing payment for repairs in excess of £67 the proposal to set (b) and (c) against (a) was approved by the Board of Inland Revenue.

It was stated that Evan's Executors held something over £6,000 in hand which, subject to the payment of expenses and costs, would be payable to the Inland Revenue. Apart from the costs of the Settled Land Act claim, the amount due for any remaining expenses or costs was not thought to be a large sum. The solicitors who acted for Evan's executors, Messrs Tozers, had been paid their costs of the general administration up to 31st March 1951.

Settled Land Claim still a Substantial Issue

The Settled Land Act claim was the one substantial matter still outstanding.

A claim for the sum of £109,000 had been initiated by Evan in his lifetime. The hope now was of being able to arrange a compromise but since that did not materialize any claim now under the Act was a matter for the discretion of a Judge. The Trustees did not consider they had power to compromise.

Earlier Blatch had warned the Board that this estimate of £109,000 was an optimistic view of the return. Messrs Tozers had advised that at best an estimated sum of £50,000 was due, allowing on the one side for the flaws in the original calculations and on the other side for extending the claim up to Evan's death.

Blatch had previously informed the Board of Inland Revenue that, in view of the Trustees' unwillingness to compromise, Counsel would be consulted and an action set in motion. Accordingly a barrister, Mr. J H Stamp[360], had been instructed by Messrs Tozers and since that time the proceedings had been conducted under his opinion, advice and directions. See the End Note and paragraph below regarding the case going before Mr. Justice Roxburgh[361] one of the most feared Chancery Judges of the 20th century.

In accordance with Mr. Stamp's advice the accounts for the purpose of the court action were recast and as a result a new Originating Summons was taken out by the Executors claiming a total sum of £60,284.8s.5d against the Trustees of the Tredegar Settled Land which it was admitted was already (for calculation purposes) been sent the net sum received under the Mineral Compensation Claim. This net sum was therefore known (i.e. the £13,423.4s.0d. referred to above as a payment) so that the maximum claim was nearly £47,000.

Objections from the Settled Land Trustees for Sums Omitted

Unfortunately when the accounts were sent to the Trustees and submitted by them to their Accountants, objections were made to them which substantially reduced the Executors' claim. The first objection resulted from the fact that a payment was made to Evan of £17,000 which had not been known about and had therefore been omitted; this payment was not notified to Evan's Executors or their professional advisors until March 1951 – i.e. after the accounts had been prepared and a new Summons against the Trustees taken out.

The second objection related to a sum of £13,374 arising in relation to the allowance of estate duty interest in computing the surtax liabilities deducted in the accounts. Both Blatch and Mr. Stamp thought that this second objection was a valid one. Taking into account some counter adjustments in favour of the Executors amounting to £3,545, the claim fell to be reduced by approximately £26,000 to the sum of £21,032.

Blatch had previously pointed out in his reports in 1949 that the Inland Revenue's net benefit from this action could not exceed 25% of the sum recovered, since the amount recovered would be deductible in arriving at the value of the Settled Estates at Evan's death in respect of which Estate Duty at 75% was payable.

Case Heard in Court by Mr. Justice Roxburgh in July, 1952

The action involving the claims against the Settled Land Trustees came before Mr. Justice Roxburgh in July 1952. His Lordship proved to be in a most difficult mood. Counsel for the Trustees did his best to assist Counsel for the Executors in overcoming some of the Judge's requirements and objections, resulting in the unexpected position that the Trustees were not seriously opposing the claim though they, of course, drew the Judge's attention to matters that were relevant to the exercise of his discretion. Although the accounts on which the claim was based were accepted on behalf of the Trustees the Judge, among other things, required to be satisfied that each item of expenditure fell within the Act. The Judge's list of requirements had been prepared by Messrs Tozers

In effect, so far as the Revenue was concerned there was a maximum of £5,000 at issue. The claim for £21,032 was a matter for the Judge's discretion and, in exercising his discretion, he was likely to consider that the claim was to benefit Evan's creditors. While technically this should not affect the claim (a view shared by the Inland Revenue and their Counsel) the matter had to be decided by the Judge.

In addition, in the figures on which the claim was based, a sum of £16,000 was suggested as a reasonable sum by Mr. Stamp to be included for Evan's personal living expenses for the period of the claim. This sum was possibly a controversial item and it was thought might well serve to reduce the amount, if any, that would be recovered.

Whilst all these points had at all times been known about, they had naturally assumed more importance with the dwindling of the sum involved and with the initial rebuff with which the claim has met at Mr. Justice Roxburgh's hands.

Reversionary Interest on Courtenay Morgan's Estate

A further matter for consideration in deciding on the Inland Revenue's attitude to this claim arose in connection with the contingent reversionary interest in the Tredegar Settled Estates.

In effect, if John Morgan, the present tenant-for-life, left no male issue (in 1952 John was aged 44 and still a bachelor) these estates (in respect of Courtenay and Evan, the last two Viscounts) might well serve to make the entire estate solvent subject to Estate Duty and to the payment of Surtax still owing by the late Viscount Courtenay Morgan (Evan's father, who died in 1934 owing Surtax arrears of £87,000[362]). In that case the Board of Inland Revenue would receive the whole of the arrears of Surtax due.

This was a bizarre complication. Moreover, if the contingent reversionary interest (in the Settled Estates) was not sold it was noteworthy that if it fell into possession, the Settled Estate against which the Executors were claiming would become the property of the Executors. If the interest did fall into possession, the only advantage from the present claim, assuming that it was successful, was therefore be one of time. That issue was however, all very much a matter of speculation.

The claim of Evan's Executors and the costs were the costs of the Executors but, as the Inland Revenue were now the only creditors of the Estate, the Executors were to some extent dependent upon the views of the Board of Inland Revenue and in deciding whether to continue the action they would no doubt be influenced by the Board's wishes. So far as the beneficiaries of Evan's estate were concerned (for instance Buckfast Abbey) there could, it seems, be no advantage to them in continuing the action for they could not hope to benefit under Evan's Will unless and until the contingent reversionary interest fell into the possession of the Executors.

One of the Executors, Mr. Edwards, was due to attend a meeting with the Solicitor of Inland Revenue. It was considered that the best course to progress matters was to restore the case to the Law List with the minimum of further information and let the Judge deal with matters as seemed fit.

Evan's Erotic Bronze Statuette by Rodin

On 12th December 1952 it was reported that the Inland Revenue had received a letter from Messrs Tozers concerning a statuette by Rodin owned by Evan which had not yet been disposed of by the Executors. The item was subject to a request in Evan's Will that read "To the Louvre Museum at Paris my erotic bronze statuette of Satyr by A. Rodin".

It was considered that the proceeds of the sale of the statuette would be available for discharge of the tax debt to the Revenue but it was, in law, the property of the Executors. Therefore the suggestion was made that some attempt should be made to sell it, with the agreement of the Executors being obtained before any offer was accepted. The name of Mr. Wyn Griffith, one of the members of the Board of Inland Revenue, was cited as a member of the Arts Council.

The papers record that "He [Griffith] might possibly be able to form some estimate of the artistic merits and value of the statuette and to suggest methods of disposal".

Subsequently the papers explain that the figurine was valued by Messrs Sotheby's as worth £32.10s.0d. Sotheby's commented that the minor works of Rodin did not command high prices so the Inland Revenue decided that they did not wish to interfere in the matter of the disposal of the statuette.

VII

Account from Tozers

The Inland Revenue files indicate that on 16th July 1954 Tozers were in the process of calculating their account in respect of Mr. Edwards' involvement in the matter of Evan's last affairs. The estimate for this, covering the period from April 1949 to June 1954, was 650 guineas excluding disbursements. The account was approved by the Inland Revenue and paid by the Executors.

Final Stages

By late 1954 the administration of Evan's last affairs had reached a stage whereby the Executors had rendered an account which it was hoped would virtually close the administration apart from a few small items. The Solicitor of Inland Revenue received the account, which gave details of the receipts and payments by the Executors from the date of Evan's death up to 1st December 1954. The accounts were scrutinized carefully and it was decided that the details could be approved by the Inland Revenue.

On 8th December 1954 two minor points were raised with Messrs Tozers, the solicitors for the executors. The first concerned Evan's debts where the Inland Revenue asked for confirmation that no further debts would be payable as some of the items included in the Inland Revenue affidavit were not included in the account or were more than the amounts included in the account. The second point related to a receipt for a sum still to be paid and therefore was not covered by the account.

A few further matters remaining outstanding were listed as follows relating to assets:-

1. The Post War Credits of the Deceased

It was considered that unless there was some means by which these could be set off against the arrears of surtax the sums due would have to be held until under the existing legislation they could be redeemed when the deceased would have reached 65. It was envisaged that Evan's Executors would agree to an immediate set off and the

Solicitor asked the Board whether they wished such an agreement to be entered into.

2. £250 Phyllis Court Members' Ltd 4½% Debentures

Evan held shares in a club on the River Thames called Phyllis Court but it had proved difficult for his Executors to sell these shares.

The Revenue papers record "No purchasers for these debentures [in Phyllis Court] can be found and in the meantime the Executors continue to hold them and to receive the interest under deduction of tax."

Subsequently (after a prolonged correspondence) a prospective buyer came forward who offered to produce a small additional sum to absorb into Evan's assets for disposal[363] but this offer was rejected. Latterly the Inland Revenue papers indicate that the debentures in Phyllis Court Members Club were transferred to the Executors of Evan's Estate. These shares were then by title offered to the Inland Revenue in order to collect any dividends.

3. Income Apportioned of the Settled Estates

There was a sum of £2,051.16s.1d due to Evan's Executors in respect of income apportionments up to the 31st December 1953. This sum would be released shortly and would increase the cash in the hands of the Executors to a little under £5,500. There might be further income apportionments still to come but it was not expected that they would be substantial amounts.

4. Loss or Damage to Heirlooms.

It was reported that from time to time Messrs Rider Heaton & Co., acting for the Trustees of the Tredegar Settled Estates, had intimated that a possible claim might be made against the Executors in respect of loss or damage to heirlooms. No specific claim had yet been made and owing to the lapse of time it was viewed as very difficult for such a claim to be substantiated. This was particularly so regarding any question of damage, in that the existing heirlooms had been removed to storage and it was therefore thought to be very difficult to prove that any damage had been done for which Evan was personally liable prior to his death in April 1949.

5. Reversionary Interest

There was the possibility of Evan's final estate benefitting from the reversionary interest in the Settled Lands Estates which would fall into the estate of his father, Courtenay, should John Morgan have no male issue.

John Morgan and his wife proposed living permanently abroad.

Another related set-off was deemed possible in respect of provision made in previous Tredegar family legacies in respect of a Miss Violet Sidney,[364] who survived Evan.

6. Sum to meet any future costs.

The Inland Revenue Solicitor thought this was a good suggestion, particularly as it was not possible to forecast what expenditure might be necessary in relation to the contingent reversionary interest referred to above. Authorization was therefore given to retain £500, to be placed on deposit (as suggested by Messrs Tozers) and treated as a reserve, pending the Board's agreement.

7. Income Tax liabilities

Messrs Tozers suggested to the Inland Revenue that a calculation should be made of the amounts still owing by Evan's estate in respect of his tax liabilities. The Executors' detailed account showed the cash payments and set-offs that the Revenue had received from this estate. The cash payments were those referred to in the course of correspondence plus an additional payment of £3,500 received subsequently, and the set-off in respect of the Income Tax maintenance claim was also confirmed by previous statements. The small amounts of set-off were also to be confirmed.

8. Surtax summary and Special Contribution

The full amount of the surtax liability was agreed with Messrs Tozers to be £246,753.18s.3d., to which £6,496 had to be added in respect of a Special Contribution. A technical query was raised on the position relating to the Special Contribution but it was thought it should apply as a charge against the Capital of the Settled Estates. This issue was one for the Special Commissioners.

Progress was ongoing, since the extent to which the estate had been administered meant that payments and set-offs received generally on account could now be properly allocated against the various items of liability.

Once these allocations were approved by the Board of Inland Revenue Messrs Tozers were notified of the overall position.

It was noted that Messrs Tozers' general costs were still to be billed and approved. The Inland Revenue had received approximately £126,000 against Evan's Surtax arrears and a small part of this sum, some £3,000, was due to be allocated to Estate Duty in respect of the liability of the Marriage Settlement Funds received on the death of Katharine (Evan's mother). Excluding the Special Contribution, a sum roughly equal to half the surtax liability had been settled leaving the other half and any interest payable on the various liabilities still outstanding.

8. Surtax Adjustments

By 1955-56 matters relating to Evan's estate were still not fully resolved. At the outset (in 1949, at Evan's death) the Revenue's claim was for surtax of more than £250,000. In 1955 the Revenue's case papers indicate that the arrears then stood at £122,803.10s covering the tax years 1940/41 to 1949/50.

In 1955 Evan's cousin, John Morgan, had succeeded his late father as the Sixth Baron Tredegar. John was tenant for life of The Tredegar Settled Estates, valued at £2,500,000 in 1949. After taxation (death duties) this would be considerably reduced.[365]

The Inland Revenue papers record that "If he [John] leaves no male heir who attains the age of twenty-one, then the absolute interest in possession will revert to the estate of the first Viscount [Courtenay Morgan] who died in 1934. A substantial claim for surtax was made against [Courtenay's] estate: it was not met in full but only a nominal sum of about £10,000 was shown to be outstanding."

Determined to receive every penny the Revenue Solicitor records:

"The balance [payable] can, of course, be restored should it be necessary to do so. If the family fortunes revert to the first Viscount's estates and they are more than sufficient to meet demands for death duties and surtax the balance will pass to the estate of the second Viscount [Evan] where it will be subject to similar demands. If anything remains after the debts of the two Viscounts are cleared, the residue will pass to Buckfast Abbey."

This concept of allocating the reversionary interest hit a problem when it was revealed that John Morgan (on advice from his lawyers) had bought the interest in question.[366] The papers show that the Inland Revenue was previously consulted about the purchase.

The Inland Revenue papers record: "The reference to the possible reversion of the interest to Courtenay Morgan's estate [first Viscount Tredegar] was taken from the historical papers, but subsequently it was discovered that the story went further as John Morgan had already bought the interest in 1955. Accordingly there was no further tax recoverable from Courtenay Morgan's estate to usefully be set off against Evan's estate".

The same conclusion was reached in respect of the estate of Miss Violet Sidney.

VIII

Post War Credits and Closure

The Inland Revenue file contains a reference to how Post War Credits (due to Evan at age 65) were dealt with to reduce the overall tax debt.

"In the normal case we cannot set off Post War Credits against tax arrears. Where there is an insolvency, however (including an insolvent estate of a deceased person), different considerations apply following Section 31 of the Bankruptcy Act 1914. Because of the 'family' considerations we are not treating this estate as an insolvent one in strictness, but the administrative nuisance of keeping the comparatively small amount of Post War Credits out of the settlement is hardly justified, and I agree with the Assessments Division that we should apply the insolvency principle in this respect at least. "

There was one small adjustment: "While agreeing that the rateable set-off is the right one, I do not think any objection need be raised if in the course of working out the final figures some other method of apportionment is found to be convenient. The amount is so very small in relation to the arrears."

Final threads and Closure

In the final throes of settling Evan's last affairs much work had been done by Edwards of Tozers. It seems ironic that since Tozers was essentially representing the interests of Buckfast Abbey, the monks of that hallowed establishment (which was dear to Evan's heart) received nothing from Evan's final legacy. There is evidence to suggest that a donation was sent to Buckfast Abbey in lieu of monies due from Evan's Will and sentiments.

One of the last entries in the Inland Revenue papers is this request to draw a line under the case:

"The tax still due from the estate is £122,803 and there seems to be no likelihood that we may recover anything but an exceedingly small fraction of this. Having in mind the need to show in the Arrears list a realistic picture of the surtax debt we hope to recover, I think that a considerable part of the tax due from the estate should be remitted as irrecoverable under Class 3. This item will appear prominently on the Board's Remission List and I should therefore be glad of your authority to write off £122,500 of the debt .... Anything recovered in excess of the amount left in charge could be brought to account as "duty unassessed".

The successive Solicitors of Inland Revenue had almost exclusively administered the inner workings of their department towards settling Evan's last affairs.[367] It had taken almost nine years hard labour.

There are a few loose papers relating to Evan's last estate in the period 1958-1961. These contain the final proceeds of various gatherings-in by Evan's executors of small sums, including the final remittance of apportionments of income from the Tredegar Settled Lands. The final small account form Tozers is dated 17 March 1960. The final entry on the file relates to the disposal of the shares in Phyllis Court Club, dated 30 August 1961. The date the papers were finally "PUT AWAY" (a term for filing away in the Archives) was 25th January 1962.

END NOTES

[1]According to Thomas Nichols' 'Annals and Antiquities of the Counties and County Families of Wales Volume 2 (1872)' : the Morgan Crest was " a reindeer's dead couped or, attired gu." Hence the style of the livery button.

[2]The Cincinnati Enquirer,12 December, 1920.

[3]Caerleon was a centre of Roman occupation from 75 to 300AD.

[4] http://www.caerleon.net/history/arthur/page7.htm

[5]The Cincinnati Enquirer,12 December, 1920.

[6]From 'The Book of South Wales, the Wye and the Coast': Samuel Carter 1861.

[7]Hastings, Selina. 'The Red Earl- The Extraordinary Life of the 16th Earl of Huntingdon. ' Bloomsbury (2014).

[8]Ash, Stephen J. 'Black Knights.' Lulu (2008). The author had the great pleasure of meeting Steve Ash in London in 2013 during and after a talk about Evan Morgan and Aleister Crowley given by William Cross and Monty Dart at Treadwell's Bookshop.

[9] Aleister Crowley (1875-1947). Poet, priest and satanist. Evan knew Crowley over a number of decades. In 1943 the Great Beast (as Crowley was known) stayed for a few days at Tredegar House. During the stay Crowley saw Evan's magic room where black mass was held. See Cross, William. ' Not Behind Lace Curtains' Book Midden Publishing: The Hidden World of Evan, Viscount Tredegar' (2013).

[10]Ash. Stephen J. 'Black Knights.' Lulu (2008).

[11]Ibid.

[12]'A Beautiful Nuisance', ISBN 9781905914104; 'Aspects of Evan', ISBN 9781905914159; and 'Not Behind Lace Curtains', ISBN 9781905914210.

[13]Executors details: The Right Honourable Evan Frederick Viscount Tredegar, deceased. Testator died at Honeywood House, Oakwood Hill, Dorking, Surrey on 27th April 1949.Grant of Probate, save and except Settled Land, issued out of Principal Probate Registry on the 29th December 1949. Executors :- The Right Honourable Charles Alexander, Earl of Southesk, K.C.V.O off Kinnaird Castle, Brechin, Angus Scotland.,Major Raymond Alexander Carnegie of Crimonmogate Loumay, Aberdeenshire, Scotland and Theodore Henry Edgcome Edwards Esq of 2 Orchard Gardens, Teignmouth, Devon. Power reserved to the Right Honourable Theobald Walter Somerset, Earl of Carrick. NOTE: The Estate, being insolvent, was administered under the directions of the Board of Inland Revenue.

[14]Lowndes. Susan [Ed]. 'Diaries and Letters of Marie Belloc Lowndes. 1911-1947.' Chato & Windus. (1971). Diary entry for 22 September 1946

[15]Ibid.

[16] Ibid.

[17] In 1923 Evan's Mother's half- brother, Charles, Lord Carnegie married Princess Maud Duff, granddaughter of King Edward VII.

[18]Prince George, Duke of Kent died in a mysterious plane crash in 1942. Evan and the Prince were sometimes in each other company in the 'Bright Young Things' era.

[19]This episode is described in detail by Robin Bryans in his books of memoir and by William Cross in 'Not Behind Lace Curtains. The Hidden World of Evan, Viscount Tredegar.' Book Midden Publishing .(2013).

[20]Robin Bryans (1928-2005). Travel-writer, poet, author of several volumes of autobiography and memoir. Bryans was a close friend of Evan from 1944 until 1949. Bryans first reflects on meeting Evan in his early work 'The Protégé' (published in 1963) writing under the name of Robert Harbinson.

[21]Bryans. Robin. 'The Dust Has Never Settled.' Honeyford Press. (1992). According to Bryans the Queen tried to take steps to have the photographs held by Evan seized and destroyed. The police visited Evan at Honeywood House and removed some property from his dark room. Evan was subsequently cautioned about the matter of hoarding indecent images of males.

[22]Bryans, Robin. ' The Dust Has Never Settled' Honeyford Press(1992).

[23]The newspapers of time said Evan's death was from ' continental flu' since death from cancer was seen as a stigma. Evan's death certificate gives the causes as (a) Acute Bronco pneumonia; (b) General carcinomatosis; (c) Primary carcinoma of the Pancreas. Certified by G De Lacey, FRCS.

[24] Robin Bryans comments in 'The Dust Has Never Settled' "Under Attlee's influence Evan made numerous improvements on his own and other East End estates, and that was why, when royalty shunned the disgraced Evan's funeral, the Labour Prime Minister Attlee sent a representative..." Evan stood against Attlee at the 1929 General Election in Limehouse.

[25]The Times, 9thMay, 1949. Requiem Mass held on Saturday 7 May, 1949 at Farm Street Church [Mayfair] by Father CC Martindale. Evan's funeral took place at Buckfast Abbey, Devon on Monday 2 May, 1949.

[26]This is how Robin Bryans describes Henry Maxwell.

[27]Henry Maxwell (1909-1996). Writer and long term lover of Evan. According to Robin Bryans in' The Dust Has Never Settled'.. " ..after coming down from Cambridge Henry started his long affair with Evan Tredegar." Bryans also recalls liaisons between Evan and a Northern Irish aristocrat named Peter Montgomery (1909-1988), also cited as a lover of the spy Anthony Blunt. Peter's brother Father Hugh Montgomery was also attached to the Vatican and knew Evan there in the 1930s.

[28]Bryans, Robin. 'The Dust Has Never Settled.' Honeyford Press. (1992). Bryans points out that among those who made his point about Evan and

Henry was Alice Pethybridge of Cardiff (who died in 1969, aged 103) and who knew Evan all his life, she was a close friend of Evan's Stewart-Carnegie relations. The impetus in the affair was always from Henry who also had gay relationships with Peter Montgomery and Prince Chula of Siam, the motor racing driver. Evan accepted invitations to Prince Chula's Phya Thai Palace when he travelled in the Far East. Henry fell out with Evan from time to time, he is described by Bryans as " the jealous type" and resented Evan taking up with boyfriends " that lasted 2 or 3 months" [Source :paper in Tredegar Archives] and spending time with Bosie Douglas and Bryans. Maxwell fully expected that Evan would leave him Honeywood House.

[29]Cyril Hughes Hartmann (1896-1967). Writer,Poet and Historian. A good friend and correspondent with Evan from their Oxford days onwards. A tranche of the letters from Evan to Cyril from 1916-1925 (approx) is held in the Tredegar Archives at Tredegar House. Sadly, by the time (in the mid 1970s) that the first Tredegar House curators were making soundings and gathering information among Evan's close friends, Cyril was dead.

[30] Charges could be brought for buggery or attempted buggery under ' The Offences Against the Person Act, 1861' and for gross indecency under 'The Criminal Law Amendment Act , 1885.' See Cross, William. 'The Abergavenny Witch Hunt. An account of the prosecution of over twenty homosexuals in a small Welsh town in 1942.' Book Midden Publishing. (2014).

[31] See Bryans, Robin. 'Checkmate: Memoirs of a Political Prisoner.' Honeyford Press. (1994). Bryans left Britain soon after Evan's death and lived in Canada with Lord George Rodney, another of Evan's early band of followers from Eton College onwards. Whilst Bryans cites John Morgan the first on the scene were Evan's Executors and in particular his Carnegie cousins, who also had control over settling Katharine's affairs in life and death.

[32]Lady Katharine Agnes Blanche Carnegie (1867-1949). Daughter of James Carnegie 9th Earl of Southesk and his second wife, Susan Murray of Kinnaird Castle. Brechin. She married Courtenay Charles Evan Morgan in 1890. There were two children from the marriage, Evan (1893-1949) and Gwyneth (1895-1924). Katherine was the second Lady Tredegar (1913-1926); Viscountess Tredegar (1926-1934) and Dowager Viscountess Tredegar (1934-1949).

[33] In his will Evan described himself as "an oblate of St Mary's Abbey, Buckfast". After various legacies he left the residue of his estate to the Abbey " for general charitable purposes of the community of Benedictine monks." He also desired that a Mass be said each week for seven years from the date of his death.

[34]Desmond Arthur Peter Leslie (1921-2010). Writer and film maker. Youngest son of Shane Leslie and Marjorie Ide. Subject of the biography ' Desmond

Leslie : the Biography of an Irish Gentleman' by Robert O' Byrne. The Lilliput Press Ltd. (2010).

[35]Letter dated 22 October, 1992 from Desmond Leslie to David Freeman (then Curator at Tredegar House). This was almost certainly how Evan's last days were described by others to Desmond to provide something of a 'feel good factor' about how a much beloved figure in his life went bravely to his grave.

[36]From 1951 until 1973 Tredegar House was owned by St Joseph's Convent School. From 1973 onwards it was the responsibility of Newport Town (later City) Council. In 2012 The National Trust negotiated a 50-year lease on the house and 90 acre site.

[37]Bryans. Robin. 'The Dust Has Never Settled.' Honeyford Press. (1992).

[38]Lowndes. Susan [Ed]. Diaries and Letters of Marie Belloc Lowndes. 1911-1947. Chato & Windus. (1971). Diary entry for 22 September 1946.

[39]The poem is reproduced in Cross, William. 'Not Behind Lace Curtains.' Book Midden Publishing. (2013).

[40]Morgan, Katharine Agnes Blanche. ' The Crimson Ducks. A book for children.' With illustrations. (1903).

[41] Hon. Gwyneth Ericka Morgan (1895-1924). See Cross, William and Dart Monty. 'A Beautiful Nuisance : The Life and Death of the Hon. Gwyneth Ericka Morgan.' Book Midden Publishing. (2012).

[42]See Cross, William. 'Not Behind Lace Curtains. The Hidden World of Evan, Viscount Tredegar.' Book Midden Publishing (2013).

[43] See Pryce-Jones, Alan. ' The Bonus of Laughter.' Hamish Hamilton (1987).

[44]See Marks Howard. ' Senor Nice: Straight Life from Wales to South America.' Random House. (2010). The author of this book refers to a trip around Tredegar House when Evan's mother was recalled by one of the guides " His [Evan's] mother was even more an eccentric [than him]. She built bigger and bigger bird's nests in the house and ended up living in one of them." See also the otherwise excellent David Conway's: 'Magic Without Mirrors: The Making of a Magician. 'Logios Publishing (2011) that author says of the Morgans " ..the Morgan family had quite a thing about birds, with Evan's mother....from time to time persuaded she was one herself. When that happened, she would go out into the grounds and build a large nest of sticks and mud then install herself inside it, cooing prettily at all who chanced to stroll by." [These stories have all the components of mischievous commentaries entirely fiction. Katharine hardly ever set foot in Tredegar House, she couldn't stand her husband Courtenay or Wales, they lived apart almost all the 44 years they were married. It is recorded that a large nest was once specially built and displayed as an exhibit at Tredegar House, purporting to be one that Katharine built and sat in. Visitors were fooled and Katharine's memory humiliated. A former Curator of the House confirms the nest was actually

made by the Newport Council gardeners. The National Trust are the current caretakers of the house and are aiming that volunteers (who now tell stories of the house and its past incumbents to visitors) offer only facts that are true and proven.

[45]Lady Emerald Cunard (1872-1948). American born Maud Burke: her daughter Nancy adored black men and Evan.

[46] Fielding, Daphne Vivian. 'Those Remarkable Cunards: Emerald and Nancy.' Atheneum. (1968)

[47]Carter, Angela. 'The Curious Room. Collected Dramatic Works.' Random House. (2013).

[48] Ibid.

[49] Aldous Huxley (1894-1963). English writer. Friend and companion of Evan Morgan at Oxford and in London.

[50]Huxley, Aldous. 'Letters of Aldous Huxley.'Harper and Row. (1970).

[51]Frances Stevenson (1888-1972). Secretary and Mistress of politician and Prime Minister David Lloyd George, later his second wife.

[52]David Lloyd George (1863-1945). Welsh and British Politician, Prime Minister of Britain (1916-1922) and Statesman.

[53] See Campbell, John. 'If Love Were All: The Story of Frances Stevenson and David Lloyd George.' Random House. 2007.

[54]Ibid.

[55]Cecil Roberts. 1892-1976). British Writer and Journalist.

[56]Roberts, Cecil. 'The Bright Twenties.'Hodder & Stoughton Ltd (1974).

[57]Lowndes. Susan [Ed]. Diaries and Letters of Marie Belloc Lowndes. 1911-1947. Chato & Windus. (1971). Diary entry for 22 September 1946.

[58]Liberty saw service in the North Sea off the Belgium and French coast and in the Mediterranean, it was able to take over 800 wounded soldiers and sailors. One of its first sea engagements was off Heligoland when Liberty picked up many German casualties, see The New York Times, 30 August 1914. The Washington Post from 14[th]January 1917 carries a tribute to Courtenay: " Another instance of the patriotism of England's wealthiest class has come to public notice after having been kept a military secret by the war office for two years. Lord Tredegar, it develops, only a few days after war was declared, turned/over the Liberty, his palatial steam yacht Liberty to the naval authorities for use as a hospital. Within ten days the fleet pleasure vessel was transformed into one of the most luxurious and most completely equipped of the floating hospitals in Great Britain's service."

[59]Prince Arthur of Connaught (1883-1938). In 1913 he married Princess Alexandra of Fife. In 1923 Alexandra's sister Princess Maud married Lord Charles Carnegie, half nephew of Evan's mother Katharine. Alexandra and Maud were granddaughters of King Edward VII.

[60] A dark cloud hung over London following the death of Sir Denis Anson (1888-1914) a Society friend of Evan's who had drowned during a boozy party on a boat on The Thames on 3 July, 1914. This tragedy blighted merriment and celebrations among Anson's contemporaries. As war was imminent this is also given as a reason for Evan's 21st birthday not being marked except informally. The Morgan tenants did make a presentation to him as the Tredegar heir in waiting.

[61]There was a appearance by Evan back in Newport at Xmas time of 1914. The Western Mail of 22 December, 1914 refers to the opening of a series of clubs for wives and dependents of soldiers and sailors. Evan's relation Mrs Leolin Forestier Walker asked Evan to open ' Herber Villa, Gold Tops ' Newport. The premises were expected to open from 9 am till 9 pm daily and provide reading and recreation rooms for adults and children.

[62]Aldous Huxley (1894-1963). Novelist, poet and drug user. Captured Evan in fiction as Ivor Lombard in his first successful book " Crome Yellow" (a parody on his Garsington Manor days).

[63]http://www.theparisreview.org/interviews/4698/the-art-of-fiction-no-24-aldous-huxley

[64]Evan's poems "In Olden Days" and "A Serenade" appeared in the 1917 edition of Oxford Poetry.

[65]The Nineteenth Century and After. Volume 80. Leonard Scott Publishing Company. (1916).

[66]'Soldier Poets : songs of the fighting men.' Erskine Macdonald, London (1916). Two of Evan's poems ' What of the Dead?' and ' The World's Reward : To NS, 1st Coldstream Guards' appear here.

[67]'The Bookman.' Hodder and Stoughton. (1917).

[68] See Graves, Robert. 'In Broken Images. Selected Letters of Robert Graves.' Hutchinson (1982).

[69]Brooke was so described by the Irish poet, W B Yeats.

[70]Garsington Manor, near Oxford was the home of the Society hostess Lady Ottoline Morell (1873-1938). Rupert Brooke was at Garsington regularly in the period before he went to war and died of blood poisoning. Evan's recorded appearances by Garsington regulars by Virginia Woolf, Lytton Strachey, and Aldous Huxley appear to be start c 1916, - that is after Brooke was long dead.

[71]Evan makes reference to " poor Rupert Brooke" in a letter to Cyril Hughes Hartmann (censor opening dated 26 February 1916).

[72]Sir Edward Marsh (1872-1953). Patron of the Arts and sponsor of the Georgian poets, like Brooke. Marsh was private secretary to a succession of Prime Ministers ; he was known to favour his fellow homosexuals.

[73]Woolf, Virginia. 'The Letters of Virginia Woolf.' Volume 2. Hogarth Press. (1976).

[74]Holroyd. Michael. 'Lytton Strachey : A Critical Biography: The years of achievement 1910-1932.' Holt, Rinehart and Winston. (1968).

[75] Osmond Thomas Grattan Esmonde, twelfth baronet (1896–1936) of Ballynastragh.

[76] Esmonde was born at Gorey, Co. Wexford, Ireland on 4 April 1896 and educated at Downside Abbey and Balliol College, Oxford, where he was a pupil of the Catholic tutor F. F. Urquhart.. Active in Sinn Féin from 1918, he was a republican envoy to the USA and the dominions in 1920–21 (thus following his father's example as an Irish nationalist envoy). He was refused permission to disembark in Australia, in March 1921, following his refusal to take the oath of allegiance and loyalty to the crown, and was subsequently deported from Canada after being arrested for 'sedition' in Vancouver. He was Cumann na nGaedheal and Fine Gael TD for Wexford from 1923 to 1927 and again, after a short interval, from 1927 until his death. In 1927 he became estranged from his father, who complained that he had taken to drink. In May 1933, in a publicity stunt to ridicule De Valera's rural policy and the Irish government's proposal to remove the statue of Queen Victoria from outside Leinster House in Dublin, Esmonde placed a wreath of cauliflowers and leeks at the foot of the statue, accompanied by a fellow Cumann na nGaedheal TD wearing a peasant smock and holding a bunch of rhubarb to represent a mace. He was later allegedly involved with Francis Stuart in a harebrained plot to stage a coup and install a member of the O'Neill family as king of Ireland, but this progressed very little beyond fantasy. Latterly in poor health, he died suddenly of a heart attack in Dublin on 22 July 1936, less than three weeks after the high court upheld his father's will. As he was unmarried, the baronetcy passed to his uncle, [From Patrick Maume in the Oxford Dictionary of National Biography].

[77]Letter in Tredegar House Archives, dated 25 July 1916 from Evan to Cyril Hughes Hartmann.

[78]Letter in Tredegar House Archives, post mark dated 28 July 1916 from Evan to Cyril Hughes Hartmann.

[79]Letter in Tredegar House Archives, dated 25 June 1917 from Evan to Cyril Hughes Hartmann.

[80]Letter in Tredegar House Archives, dated 10 July 1917 from Evan to Cyril Hughes Hartmann.

[81] Home of the Esmonde family. The Irish Times of , 12th March 1923, states: "Ballynastragh, the beautiful residence of Senator Sir Thomas Henry Grattan Esmonde, Bart., about three miles from Gorey, County Wexford, was set on fire on Friday night, and burned to the ground."

[82] Sir Kenelm Lister- Kaye (1892-1955). Of Denby Grange, Near Flockton, Wakefield. Later Mullingar Estate and Co West Neath, Ireland. Kenelm was

the brother of Adeline de la Feld, a close friend of Evan and life-long contact of Robert Bryans. Another of Kenelm's sisters was Francis (1882-1984), the mother of Bridget and Desmond Parsons, who were two charismatic (although doomed) members of the Bright Young Things brigade.

[83]A description by Robin Bryans in 'The Dust Has Never Settled.' Honeyford Press (1992).

[84] Kenelm took part on the famous Fowler match between Eton and Harrow in 1910. www.espncricinfo.com/magazine/content/story/248116.html

[85]James Lonsdale Bryans (1893-1981). Met Evan at Eton. They saw each other from time to time (especially in Germany in the 1930s).

[86]Peter Spencer Churchill, knew Evan from 1901 onwards at Windsor Castle. Later 2nd Viscount Churchill, died 1973.

[87]Bryans, Robin. 'The Dust Has Never Settled.' Honeyford Press (1992).

[88] Kenelm's mother was Lady Beatrice Pelham-Clinton (1862-1935) daughter of the 6th Duke of Newcastle, she was the sister of Lord Francis Hope (previously Pelham- Clinton) (1866-1941) who came to own the 45.53 carat Hope diamond. According to Marion Fowler in 'Hope Adventures of a Diamond' Pocket Books. (2003). Lord Francis (when bankrupt couldn't sell the stone direct) he " bribed his sister Beatrice in order to get her consent to the sale [of the diamond] and which would go " toward the education and maintenance of her six year old son [Kenelm]."

[89] Bryans, Robin. 'The Dust Has Never Settled.' Honeyford Press (1992).

[90] Ibid.

[91]Ibid.

[92] The Times of 18 June, 1915 reports" The Hon. Evan F Morgan only son of Lord and Lady Tredegar has received a Commission in the Welsh Guards and joined his regiment at Wellington Barracks last week."

[93] On 25 July, 1916 Evan wrote to Cyril Hughes Hartmann " this week's World will have 2 poems of mine in it." [Tredegar Archives.]

[94] In New Age Evan defended the rights of foreigners from abroad – and in particular Indians – being treated fairly and without any kind of discrimination. In the Letters section of the magazine there is a interesting debate started by Anglo Indian DK Sorabji (later name used Kaikhosru Shapurji Sorabji) which Evan contributed to. Sorabji was a lifelong friend and confidant of Peter Hestletine – also known as Peter Warlock (1894-1930) and one of the Effiel Tower Restaurant crowd. Sorabi became music critic of New Age. See http://www.sorabji-archive.co.uk/index.php

[95]Letter (opened by the censor 26 February 1916) from Evan to Cyril Hughes Hartmann in the Tredegar House Archives.

[96] Ibid.

[97] Letter dated 25 July 1916 from Evan to Cyril Hughes Hartmann.

[98] Western Mail, 26 August 1916.

[99] Attributed in 1913 to Leolin Forestier Walker (1866-1934). A cousin and exact contemporary of Courtenay Morgan. When Courtenay rejected standing for Parliament in 1905 (in succession to his MP father Freddie Morgan) Leolin stepped in. He was Conservative candidate (defeated in the Liberal Party landslide in the General Election of 1906) he was later and MP for Monmouthshire from 1918 until his death.

[100] Daily Mirror, 26 July, 1916.

[101] One example of this scheming was by Violet, 8th Duchess of Rutland on behalf of her son John Manners, the Marquess of Granby, heir to the Duke of Rutland who went through the same charades as Evan pretending to be a soldier and serving in Battle. See Bailey, Catherine. 'The Secret Rooms. A True Gothic Mystery.' Viking. (2012)

[102] Evan's resignation from the Welsh Guards in 1919 is represented by a letter in the Lloyd George Papers in the Parliamentary Archives (ref LG/F/8/3/35) regarding " Sir C Riddell's wish to keep Morgan in Paris for Peace Conference work."

[103] Evan was unpaid private secretary to William (later Lord) Bridgeman (1864- 1935) Parliamentary Secretary to MP John Hodge, (1855-1937) at the Ministry of Labour.

[104] Letter from Evan to Cyril Hughes Hartmann in the Tredegar Archives, undated from the year 1917.

[105] 'The Thatched House' on Selsey Bill was bought by Cyril Hughes Hartmann's father both as a seaside holiday home for his family and particularly as a healthy environment for Cyril who as a young man suffered badly from lung trouble.

[106] Letter from Evan to Cyril Hughes Hartmann in the Tredegar Archives (opened by the Censor 26th February 1916). One of the men that Evan came to befriend at Selsey wasSir Archibald Hamilton, 5th Baronet (1876-1939) of Paisley Cottage, Selsey. Hamilton later converted to the Muslim faith.
Evan writes to Cyril "I enjoyed my week end in his company immensely. Archie! – Give him my love and say when I get one moment to think I will send him the embroidery and a long epistle of thanks for his Twelve Bad Women, [a poem?] whom I beg you will "keep" until you have full use of them."

[107] Hartmann, Cyril Hughes: From " I say my Grace (unpublished memoirs, c. 1951) from the chapter entitled 'Archie and Others'. Cyril's son, the late George Hartmann presented copies of his father's letters from Evan and extracts from other letters that mentioned Evan.

[108] Letter from Evan to Cyril Hughes Hartmann in the Tredegar Archives (opened by the Censor 26 February 1916)..

[109] Letter from Evan to Cyril Hughes Hartmann in the Tredegar Archives dated 25 June 1917.

[110] Raymond Juzio Paul Rodakowski (1895- 1917). A Captain in the 1st Bn Irish Guards. A student at Oxford and friend of Cyril Hughes Hartmann at Chaterhouse School. Evan dedicated his poem ' Vale' to 'RR'. The poem is reproduced in the book ' Aspects of Evan'. Raymond's name is on the Tyne Cot Memorial, Zonnebeke, West Flanders, Belguim. Panels 10 to 11.

[111] Tommy W Earp (1892-1958). Poet, wit, critic, and ex-President of the Oxford Union.

[112] Wilfred Rowland Childe (1890-1952) . Poet and critic. Friend of JRR Tolkien. There are notes from Childe's letters to Cyril Hughes Hartmann that mention Evan from 1917-25. Childe was another who admitted [in 1916] that he was "interested in his [Evan's] personality".

[113] Letter from Evan to Cyril Hughes Hartmann in the Tredegar Archives dated 15 June 1918.

[114] Mention of Evan's conversion is often included in lists of other literary people who converted to Roman Catholic at the around the same time. 'The Catholic World' of 1932 records: " Among living Catholic converts are Alfred Noyes, Lord Alfred Douglas, Wilfred Rowland Childe, Hon. Evan Morgan, Maurice Baring, Compton Mackenzie, Shane Leslie..and Eric Gill.." all of whom interacted with Evan in the post Great War period.

[115] The Scranton Republican, 17 June, 1920.

[116] ' The Monk's Chant' was first published in The Dublin Review, Part 2 (July –December 1920).

[117] Shane Leslie (1885-1971). Irish patriot. Writer and poet.

[118] The poem was published in Evan's compilation ' At Dawn Poems Profane and Religious' Kegan Paul, Trench, Trubner &Co Ltd. (1924)

[119] Daily Mail, 24 November, 1921. The party was held on Tuesday 22nd November and Evan left for Rome on Friday 25 November 1921.

[120] Details of the relationship between Evan and Gerard Sturt is in Cross, William. ' Not Behind Lace Curtains.' Book Midden Publishing (2013).

[121] Ambrose McEvoy (1878-1927) Society painter and artist.

[122] McEvoy's painting of a young Evan Morgan is currently on display at Tredegar House, Newport.

[123] This is fully covered in Cross, William. 'Not Behind Lace Curtains. The Hidden World of Evan, Viscount Tredegar.'

[124] Firbank. Ronald. ' The Flower Beneath the Foot.' Grant Richards. (1923).

[125] Letter dated 30 January, 1921 from Katharine, Lady Tredegar to Cyril Hughes Hartmann in the Tredegar House Archives.

[126] See Cross, William and Dart Monty. 'A Beautiful Nuisance' Book Midden Publishing (2012).

[127]See the Daily Mail for 19 January 1925 and 5 July 1922.

[128] This prompted Wilfred Childe one of Evan's friends to write to Cyril Hughes Hartmann on 15 January 1925 'I have just seen a long religious poem by Evan in a Catholic paper. The tragedy of his sister was really most terrible – poor Lady Tredegar!"

[129]Margaret MacDonald (1864-1933). Scottish artist and craftswoman.

[130]Bryans. Robin. 'Checkmate: Memoirs of a Political Prisoner.' Honeyford Press (1994).

[131]Cross, William and Dart, Monty: ' A Beautiful Nuisance: The Life and Death of Hon. Gwyneth Ericka Morgan.' Book Midden Publishing (2012).

[132] Evan was court martialed in April 1943 on three counts for breaches of the Official Secrets Acts. The full transcript of the proceedings is included in Cross, William and Dart Monty. 'Aspects of Evan' Book Midden Publishing (2012).

[133] Rose Marie Antoinette Katherine (Kate) Robert de d'Aqueria de Rochegude (1874-1959). Wife of a merchant banker (Emile). A patron of the arts, and one of those who financed Cecil Beaton.

[134] Hon. Alice Grosvenor, wife of Ivor Guest, 1st Viscount Wimborne. She died in 1948.

[135]See Cross, William.' Not Behind Lace Curtains.' Book Midden Publishing (2013).

[136]http://irishcatholics.proboards.com/thread/661

[137]Bryans. Robin. ' The Dust Has Never Settled.' Honeyford Press (1992).

[138]Sir Alec Randall (1892-1977). British diplomat (Ambassador to Denmark 1947-1953). He was a 2nd Secretary to the Holy See. Author of ' Vatican Assignment Heinemann. (1956) (which refers to Evan) and other books on Rome and the Papacy.

[139]Francis D'Arcy Godolphin Osborne (1884- 1964). British Minister to the Holy See 1936-1947. Succeeded to the title of the 12th and last Duke of Leeds.

[140] In 'The Diaries of Cynthia Gladwyn'; Edited by Miles Jebb. Constable (1995) the entry for ' British Embassy, Rome , for 20 March ' 1962 reads " I lunched with D'Arcy....Always very distinguished and complicated and inhibited, one wonders what his private life and desires have really been. ...He has great friendships among women, such as the Queen Mother. And yet I think his real interest has been in young boys – the boys he used to photograph, and the boys of his adoption society. I am certain that all this is completely innocent..."

[141]Giovanni Battista Montini (1897-1978). Pope Paul VI who reigned from 1963 until 1978. Montini served in the Vatican's Secretariat of State from 1922 to 1954. Rumors have persisted that Montini had homosexual leanings.

[142] Bryans comments in 'The Dust Has Never Settled' " ...when Hugh Montgomery [brother of Evan's friend Peter Montgomery] and Mgr Montini were minor diplomats in Rome amazed at Evan's incompatible roles as Papal Chamberlain and black magician. The two well-known homosexuals from Paris, the American priest Mgr Hemmick and Sir Francis Rose never got invitations to join (Father) Hugh Montgomery at Archbishop Montini's table in Milan." Montini was Archbishop of Milan from 1954, well after Evan's death in 1949.

[143] See Randall. Sir Alec. Vatican Assignment. Heinemann (1956).

[144] Alfred Leslie Rowse (1903-1997). British historian, poet and Shakespearean scholar.

[145] Rowse, AL. 'Homosexuals in History.' Weidenfeld & Nicolson. (1977).

[146] Rowse, AL. ' A Cornishman abroad.' J Cape (1976).

[147] Connolly, Cyril and Pryce-Jones, David. ' Journal and Memoir.' Ticknor & Fields (1984) . Evan may have uplifted part of this phrase from George Bernard's Shaw's remark in a preface to his play The Doctor's Dilemma that " the sexual instinct in men is utterly promiscuous..."

[148] Evan visited Capri often including a short stay towards the end of his life. He was a friend of the Swedish guru Alex Munthe, whose villa San Michele is situated at Anacapri (on the western part of the island). The draw was that the place was an animal sanctuary. One of Evan's monkeys was reared by Munthe. There are references to this in Aspects of Evan and Not Behind Lace Curtains. Evan may have been staying with Munthe/ at San Michele in the mid late 1940s, [but he was there in the 1930s too]. When not in good health he went to Capri to get some sun and recuperate. He certainly broke the currency laws to get money wired to him to pay a local doctor c 1948. Another haunt of Evan's in Capri was the plush Quisisana Hotel – where he entertained several of his young male lovers, right up to the near end of his life. Some tales say Evan ended up in jail after being seen naked on the beach at Capri and was arrested after Gracie Fields (a famous Capri resident and English singer) saw him through her binoculars and complained. Pictures on the internet suggest Gracie's old home looks over a rocky harbour cove area beneath The joke was Gracie didn't know it was Evan's torso she observed with her spy glass / binoculars, just a rather odd looking bather wearing only a crucifix. Evan's Italian was enough to get him out of prison afterwards. (It must have just been a police cell - but Evan would have said prison!). Gracie must have known Evan / known of him/ met him as one of Gracie's great chums was Evan's drinking buddy Augustus John.

[149] Francis Mostyn (1860-1939) . Archbishop of Cardiff from 1921 to 1939. He conducted the marriage ceremony between Evan at Lois Sturt at the Brompton Oratory in 1928.

[150] "In Pace" is reproduced in full in Cross, William and Dart, Monty. ' A Beautiful Nuisance.' Book Midden Publishing (2012).

[151]Derby Daily Telegraph, 29 September 1925.

[152]Yorkshire Post, 27 March 1925

[153] Sir Lancelot Carnegie (1861-1933). Brother of Evan's mother Katharine. Lancelot was a career diplomat.

[154] See Daily Mail, 19 October 1925.

[155]Faked invitations to Evan's birthday party were sent out by pranksters. Evan got word of this and took precautions to prevent the uninvited entering the venue . The real guests had to produce different cards to the original issue. One irate guest remarked" Why didn't he insist on us bringing our birth certificates."

[156]Some narratives say that Evan was "the possessor of a plane" (see Winnipeg Tribune, 21stJanuary 1927).

[157]See Rose, Francis. ' Saying Life.' Cassell. (1961) for another (less flattering) anecdote of a meeting between Evan the Picasso when the great painter encountered Evan at play flirting with a male companion at a restaurant . Evan spotted Picasso in the room and had a drink ordered for him. Later (Picasso obviously disapproving) approached Evan's table and showered him with water from a flower vase.

[158] See The Daily Mail, 20 August, 1927.

[159] Alistair Hugh Graham (1904-1982). Alistair was the grandson of Sir Frederic Ulric Graham; his grandmother was a daughter of the 12th Duke of Somerset.

[160] Evelyn Waugh (1903-1966). English writer.

[161] http://www.evelynwaugh.org.uk/styled-6/index.html

[162] Evelyn Gardner (1903-1994). Three times married daughter of Lord and Lady Burghclere.

[163] Waugh, Evelyn. 'Brideshead Revisited', Chapman and Hall (1945)

[164]   Waugh wrote in his diary ' [Graham] Greene rang up to say that Night and Day [a magazine] is on its last legs; would I put them into touch with Evan Tredegar [2nd Viscount Tredegar], whom I barely know, to help them raise capital..."

[165] Evelyn Waugh's generation (steeped in the post WW1   20th century and the fast and furious roaring 20s) succeeded Evan's inner crowd (steeped in the pre WW1 era and the late 19th century of fops, Oscar Wilde and dark asceticism). There was an odour filled air of sharp disapproval each of the other's crowd in social intercourse and they avoided taking partners from their respective other corners for sexual encounters.

[166] There was The Savoy Turkish Bath House in Jermyn Street that Evan frequented looking for boys and men to pick up and take to the Cavendish Hotel.

[167] A description of Rosa Lewis by Evelyn Waugh "warm hearted, comic and a totally original woman, whose beauty was still discernable in old age."

[168] Rosa Lewis (1867-1952) Well known cook and hostess in Edwardian London and later years. Her grave at Putney Vale Cemetery has the words " None knew her but to love her. None named her but to praise."

[169] See Lycett, Andrew. Dylan Thomas : A New Life. Hachette. (2014). " [in New Quay Graham] "was trying to lead a respectable life, giving no indication of his scandalous past when he was run out of society following his affair with another aristocratic Welsh patron of the arts, Lord Tredegar (otherwise the poet Evan Morgan)."

[170] According for "Peerage" Graham was British Attache to Athens between 1927 and 1929 and Attache to Cairo between 1929 and 1933. Since Graham had bad debts and a number of VIP lovers who feared public exposure as he could be indiscreet, the Graham affair (leading to his exile abroad) may well have been entrapment by the Establishment to get rid of him.

[171] See Hayden. Jacki. A Map of Love: Around Wales with Dylan Thomas. Y Lolfa. (2014) " Dylan came to Gilfachreda, a short distance from New Quay, to visit Alistair Graham who lived in Plas y Wern { a large house outside New Quay]. Apart from being a regular at the Dolau [the favourite pub of Dylan's wife Caitlin] he was an oboe player and close friend of the writer Evelyn Waugh and the arts patron Lord Tredegar."

[172] Thomas, David N. The Dylan Thomas Murders. Seren. (2002).

[173] Ibid.

[174]See The Daily Mail, 22 September , 1927.

[175]The Book Review Digest, 1929.

[176]See The Illustrated London News, 4 July 1931.page 25 "Pageantry in Wales and Kent".

[177] Hon. David Tennant (1902-1968). Started the Gargoyle Club in 1925 with his actress wife Hermione Baddeley (1906-1986). According to Robin Bryans this was a favourite drop in for Evan where he entertained gay and heterosexual friends including Eddie Shackleton (1911-1994) (a Labour politician and son of the famous explorer). Bryans comments in 'Blackmail and Whitewash' that Shackleton " experienced Evan Tredegar's generosity [and took part in a black mass [when] a beautiful woman acting scarlet woman promised sexual adventures" .] 'Scarlet women' was associated with Aleister Crowley.

[178] Traded as Victor Perosino Ltd from 1924 until dissolved in 1932. See National Archives, Kew file BT31/28512/197878

[179]Kinross, Patrick, Balfour. 'Society Racket: A Critical Survey of Modern Social Life.' J Long. (1933).

[180]This coincides with a period when the Prince of Wales took charge of weaning his brother Prince George off hard drugs. Both Royal Princes and many others in their coterie were regulars at Chez Victor.

[181] Evelyn Waugh's letters in Boston University support this assertion. " 2pp. Piers Court, n.d. (1939?). To Alec Waugh. Evelyn mentions the Chez Victor in Grafton Street. Until it was closed and Victor deported for sale of drugs this was without question the leading night club."

[182]The Daily Mail (see edition of 10 December, 1927) was one newspaper to list a number of those summoned. Evan is hidden under cover of a typographical error. Evan occupied 35b Queen's Gate, London SW7 for several years. He gives this address in various publications of the Catholic Record Society 1927- 1930. Evan also lived sometime at 30 St James Place, London SW1 from 1928. He gave this address when he appealed in the newspapers for the return of a lost gold snuff box, which he noticed missing on 16 November, 1928. A reward for offered of £10 to effect its return

[183]The Police said in Court that the Club were allowed to serve alcohol only up to 11 o'clock Sundays and 12 o'clock weekdays.

[184] One of the " consumers" was the British actress Ivy St Helier (1886-1971), original star of Noel Coward's Bitter Sweet (1929). She was fined £5.00.

[185]The Club Secretary Lt Colonel Ernest English was also summoned to show cause why an order should not be made for the club to be struck off the register of companies. Subsequently the company was dissolved.

[186]Kate Meyrick (1875-1933). She went to prison five times for breaches of the drinking laws.

[187] Victor (Vittorio FA) married Lucia I Torchio in Lambeth in 1915.

[188]Aberdeen Journal, 28 January, 1929.

[189]This gave rise to a question in Parliament in 1932. The Home Office reported that Victor "was allowed to land on the 29th February[1932] for one week in order to make arrangements for the education of his British-born children and to transact certain private business." See Hansard HC Deb 07 March 1932 vol 262 c1482.

[190] Hon. Honour Chedworth Philipps (1908-1961). First married to Gavin Henderson (annulled) later married Charles Vere Pilkington. She was killed in a car accident in Spain in 1961, aged 53.

[191]Gavin Henderson (1902-1974). 2nd Lord Faringdon

[192] Daily Mail, 3 June, 1927.

[193] Daily Mail 4 June, 1927.

[194] Daily Mail 5 August, 1927.

[195]Edward William Bootle-Wilbraham, (1895-1930). 3rd and last Lord Lathom. He was also Lord Skelmersdale, that title continues to date.
[196]The usually well informed Washington Post reported on 12 September , 1920 " The engagement of Irene, daughter of the Earl of Curzon, granddaughter of Levi Leiter, and heiress to the barony of Ravensdale, to Earl Lathom will soon be announced, according to the London Express." This was repeated in the Washington Post of 19 September, 1920. Irene Curzon (1896-1966) had a number of affairs and lovers, but never married.
[197]http://george-powell.co.uk/family/1156.htm
[198]See San Francisco Chronicle, 25 November 1923.
[199] George Rodney (1891-1973). 8th Baron Rodney. A distant cousin of Evan. He was also a contemporary of Evan at Eton College. Lived most of his life in Canada where he farmed. After Evan died Robin Bryans fled to the Rodney ranch to lie low.
[200] See The Lethbridge Herald 9 February 1929. The Canadian business venture known as Oxley Ranch was between the 2nd Earl Lathom, Mr A Staveley Hill,QC, MP of Oxley Manor, Wolverhampton and a Mr J R Craig.
[201]Daily Mail, 3 June, 1927.
[202] Xenia acted in the West End of London under the name of Helen Morris. Her own name was Marie Xenia de Tunzelman. She divorced her first husband, Ronald William Morison in 1920, see National Archive file J77/1621/326. Xenia died in 1974.
[203]Daily Mail 19 March, 1927.
[204]Ned was an example of someone whose hobby became a business, He adopted the stage as his hobby, and [divided] his time between designing stage sets, writing plays [as Edward Wilbraham] , and providing exquisite [internal] decorations [and fabrics] for the houses of the rich.
[205]The Washington Post of 10 June, 1916 records "after serving as a lieutenant of the Lancashire Hussars, in Gallipoli, [Lathom] is now at the front in France". In a later edition of the same newspaper, from 26 March, 1919, the same scribe reports that Ned was in New York, with his widowed sister Lady Barbara Seymour "to recuperate from wounds received and health shattered." Ned is also recorded as being from 1916 an ADC to Lord Wallington, the Governor of Bombay. This post ended and Lathom returned to England in October, 1918.   See also The Times, 3 July 1916 and Washington Post 19 September 1920 and Oshkosh Daily Northwestern, 9 October 1918.
[206]See The Daily Mail, 17 December 1927.
[207] O.M.S. = Organisation for the Maintenance of Supplies was a British right-wing (but non-political) movement established in 1925 to provide volunteers in the event of a general strike. During the General Strike of 1926 the OMS was

taken over by the government and was used to provide vital services such as transport and communications

208See the Daily Mail, 21 December, 1927.

209Among those raising a glass to Evan and Lois were Lady Diana Cooper (who had co-starred with Lois on film), and sisters Lady Cynthia Asquith and Lady Mary Strictland. Among the men were Augustine Birrell, Lord David Cecil, Sir Philip Sassoon, the Hon. Evan Charteris , the Hon Maurice Baring and Evan's fellow Catholic poet, Hilaire Belloc.

210 Grahame Greene (1904-1991) . English Novelist. This contact with Greene and Evan was only at a distance. In 1937 on the imminent closure of the literary magazine 'Night and Day', Greene contacted Evelyn Waugh to ask him for Evan's contact details with a view to raising funds. Waugh declares on his diaries that he barely knew Evan, and it seems the rescue of the magazine in question was left too late. See Lewis. Jeremy. Shades of Greene. Random House. (2011).

211Francis McCullagh (1874-1956). British born journalist and war correspondent.

212McCullagh. Francis . 'Red Mexico.' Brentano's New York. (1928).

213Ibid.

214214 Illustrated London News, Volume 171, 1927.

215Flying Magazine for January 1930 announces that Lois (as Mrs Evan Morgan) had registered at the London Air Park at Hamworth. Other aspiring lady pilots included Lady Craven and Mrs Loel Guinness. In the May 1930 edition of the same magazine it was announced that "Lady Louis Mountbatten, Hon. Mrs Eavn Morgan, Miss Diana Guest and the Marchesa Malacreda [had] all recently taken their [pilots] licenses in Europe."

216Letter in the Tredegar House Archives from Evan to Cyril Hughes Hartmann dated approx 26 February 1916.

217Alfred Noyes (1880-1958). English poet and critic.

218Lord Alfred (Bosie) Douglas (1870-1945) . Poet, and lover of Oscar Wilde. Evan went out of his way to attract Douglas, but despite Evan's motive of wanting to bask in the glory of this gay icon, he also made Bosie's last years more bearable with gifts and in leading an attempt to secure him a Civil List pension.

219Henry 'Chips' Channon (1897- 1958) American born writer, diarist and Conservative politician.

220See Carreno, Richard. 'Lord of Hosts: The Life of Sir Henry 'Chips' Channon.' Writers Clearinghouse press.(2011). Also information to the Author from MB. Chips knew Evan from as early as 1919.

221 Spencer Churchill. John, Crowded Canvas – the Memoirs of John Spencer Churchill. Oldhams. (1961).

[222] Plimpton, George. 'Truman Capote: In which Various Friends, Enemies , Acquaintances and Detractors Recall His Turbulent Career.' Pan Macmillan (1999).

[223] Lord Louis Mountbatten (1900-1979). Killed by the IRA. Uncle of Prince Philip. Evan visited Mountbatten's homes near Southampton and in Ireland. Their paths also crossed at various places in America and Europe where the rich and famous congregated.

[224] Prince Paul of Yugoslavia (1893-1976). Oxford educated, his wife Olga was the sister of Princess Marina of Greece (who married the Duke of Kent). Closely associated with Chips Channon and dinners at Oxford's Bullingdon Club (which Evan avoided).

[225] Prince Paul of Greece, (1901-1964) from 1947 King of Greece. A constant companion of Evan on private yachting holidays. While Paul (in his early adult days) is associated with homosexual personalities, some stories of his sexual misconduct with men are described as exaggerated.

[226] Plimpton, George. 'Truman Capote: In which Various Friends, Enemies , Acquaintances and Detractors Recall His Turbulent Career.' Pan Macmillan (1999).

[227] See Daily Mail 27 May, 1929.

[228] Major Hon James Alexander Wedderburn St Clair-Erskine (1909-1973) known as Hamish St Clair Erskine was a homosexual, engaged for 5 years to the novelist Nancy Mitford she later married Hon. Peter Rodd. Erskine was described by one of his peers as "gay as gay". In those days "gay" meant a party-loving Bertie Wooster-type, but St Clair Erskine was also vehemently "gay as gay" in today's sense.

[229] Peter Watson (1908-1956) a millionaire, he was a notable art dealer and magazine patron. He drowned in his bath (some reports indicate he may have been murdered by his male lover). Later linked to the American male whore, Denham Fouts (almost certainly Fouts was a sexual conquest of Evan. See Cross, William. 'Not Behind Lace Curtains.' Book Midden Publishing (2013) and Dart, Monty and Cross William. ' Aspects of Evan.' Book Midden Publishing, (2012). NB A biography of Peter Watson is currently being written by Adrian Clark.

[230] Lady Erroll, Mrs Rosita Forbes (Mrs Arthur McGrath), Princess de Chimay and Lady Gort were among the other lunch guests.

[231] See Daily Mail, 6 June, 1929.

[232] Part of the Empire Parliamentary Association's visit to Canada as guests of The Canadian Chamber of Commerce.

[233] Derby Daily Telegraph, 23 October 1929.

[234] Ibid.

[235] Ibid.

[236]See Nottingham Evening Post, 1`3 October 1931.

[237] Yorkshire Post and Leeds Intelligencer, 17 May 1932.

[238]See Bath Chronicle and Weekly Gazette 5 March, 1932 and Aberdeen Journal 5 October, 1932.

[239] John Fothergill. (1876-1957). Proprietor of several up market pubs and hotels in the pre WW2 era.

[240]Fothergill, John. 'An Innkeeper's Diary.' The book was first published in 1931 and has rarely been out of print with several other companion editions/ titles.

[241]Ibid.

[242]Source for the cutting is The Winnipeg Tribune, 21 December, 1929.

[243] Hartmann, Cyril Hughes: From " I say my Grace (unpublished memoirs, c. 1951) from the chapter entitled 'Archie and Others'. Cyril's son, the late George Hartmann presented copies of his father's letters from Evan and extracts from other letters that mentioned Evan to Tredegar House Archives.

[244]Daily Mail, 22 July, 1921.

[245]O' Byrne Robert. ' Desmond Leslie (1921-2001). The Biography of an Irish Gentleman.' The Lippiput Press. (2010).

[246]Letter dated 22 October, 1992 from Desmond Leslie to David Freeman (then Curator at Tredegar House).

[247]Desmond Leslie says this was invented by H G Wells and Mgr Ronnie Knox (two regular stayers at Tredegar House). A game like charades there people " had to think up outrageous scenes for the rest [of the guests] to act ' In the Manner Of The Word".

[248]Evan's love of animals led to his founding a private zoo at Tredegar Park. Here was Evan's collection of strange pets including a boxing kangaroo (named Somerset) , a honey bear (named Alice) and an assortment of gorillas and birds (including flamingos on the lake at Tredegar Park) . At the outbreak of the Second World War the animals were taken in by London Zoo.

[249] Letter dated 22 October, 1992 from Desmond Leslie to David Freeman (then Curator at Tredegar House).

[250]Ibid.

[251]Desmond Leslie married Agnes Bernelle on 18 August 1945 at St James Church, Spanish Place, London. Witnesses included Evan and Beatrice Violet, Lady Leconfield as well as Desmond's parents and his brother Jack.

[252] Letter dated 22 October, 1992 from Desmond Leslie to David Freeman (then Curator at Tredegar House).

[253] Albert Martin Oppenheimer is recorded in the GRO Consular Births Indices (1871-1875) as a British National. Oppenheimer's father was honorary British Consul General at Frankfurt until 1900, when he was succeeded by another son, Sir Francis Oppenheimer, who died in 1961. In 1911 Francis (a financial

and monitory expert) was under Albert's roof at 24 Basil Street, Brompton Street, London.

[254]Death recorded in GRO Registers for July, August, September, 1945, Chelsea 1a 256.

[255] See The Times, 6 and 16 September, 1935. Gregory was groom to Courtenay Morgan. In Courtenay's will he left his clothing to Gregory and another servant. Gregory found a pair of onyx and diamond cuff links on one of the shirts and tried to sell them, he was the arrested. Evan's solicitor Oppenheimer represented Gregory and said " that Gregory had no intention of committing any theft. Not only did [Evan] intend to continue him in service, but the servant's hall would be glad to see him back." The case was dismissed.

[256]See Daily Mail, 18 January, 1930.

[257]Frank A Miller(1858-1935) . Owner and developer of Mission Inn Hotel.

[258] Gale, Zona. 'Frank Miller of Mission Inn.' D Appleton-Century company. (1938).

[259]The Brooklyn Daily Eagle, 15 March 1936.

[260] Sir Henry MORGAN pirate and administrator was born 1635, Llanrhymney, Glamorgan [now in Cardiff], Wales died August 25, 1688, probably Lawrencefield, Jamaica.

[261] Forbes, Rosita. Captain Henry Morgan. Reynal & Hitchcock. (1946).

[262] Rosita Forbes (1890-1967). Travel writer and explorer. In Evan's Oxford days when he hosted several fancy dress parties he enjoyed dressing up as Rosita. In the early 1920s she became well known for her travels in the Sahara desert ,

[263]Published by St James Press.

[264]St Bernadette of Lourdes(1844-1879). In 1925 Pope Piux XI beatified Bernardette, she was canonised by the same Pope in 1933. As a child Bernadette saw apparitions of the 'Immaculate Conception' (Mary, mother of Christ) near Lourdes. It was later ruled by the Catholic Church that these sightings were " worthy of belief".

[265]Aubrey Beardsley (1872-1898). Illustrator and Author. Evan had a large collection of Beardsley drawings in his Oxford days, that adorned his walls. He was later forced to sell them to raise funds.

[266] Huxley , Aldous. 'Letters of Aldous Huxley.' Harper and Row (1970).

[267]Duchamp, Marcel. Etant Donne. Issue No 8 (2007)

[268]See Lewis Jeremy. Cyril Connolly. A Life. Random House. 2012.

[269] This assault on Evan is described in Cross, William. 'Not Behind Lace Curtains.' Book Midden Publishing. (2013).

[270]Bryans, Robin. 'Checkmate. Memoirs of a Political Prisoner.' Honeyford Press. (1994).

[271]Ibid.

[272]Based on tales from Robin Bryans in his Memoirs.

[273]William (Billy) B Leeds Jnr was the son of William Leeds Snr, an American millionaire who had made his fortune from tin plate. Billy's mother was Princess Xenia of Greece, cousin of the last Tsar of Russia.

[274]Lady Norah Spencer Churchill (sister of the Duke of Marlborough) in The Daily Mail, 20 November, 1927.

[275]Ibid.

[276]Ibid.

[277]Attributed from the letters in the Tredegar House Archives and from an interview between the author and Alan Carnegie Stewart (a cousin of Evan). Alan's testimony on Evan is in the book 'A Beautiful Nuisance'.

[278] Rupert Mason is described by the Daily Mail as "tall, thin, and distinguished-looking and unbelievably young for his 69 years...."

[279]Robes of Thespis. Costume designs by modern artists. Edited for Rupert Mason by George Sheringham and R. Boyd Morrison, (1928).

[280]See the Daily Mail, 7 February , 1928.

[281]See Burkhart.' Hermann & Nancy & Ivy. Three Lives in Art.' Gollancz. (1977).

[282] Ibid.

[283] Catherine Stewart (1877-1975) Known as Katie or Kitty. Her mother was Lady Beatrice Stewart, half-sister of Katharine, Lady Tredegar.

[284]Princess Olga Dolgoruky (1915-1998). Daughter of Prince Serge Alexandrovitch Dolgorouky (1872-1933) and Irene Vassilievna Narychkine, (1879-1917). Olga spent her last years in the Channel Islands. Her letters (of the late 1970s) to Tredegar House formed a key element in how the early Curators restored several of the rooms including the Red Room which can still be seen in Tredegar House today.

[285]See Cross, William and Dart, Monty. 'Aspects of Evan.' Book Midden Publishing (2012).

[286] Richard Rumbold. (1913-1961). Writer and diary keeper. See Cross, William. Not behind Lace Curtains. Book Midden Publishing. (2013).

[287] Croft-Cooke. Rupert. The happy highways. W H Allen. (1967).

[288]Valentine Edward Charles Browne, 6th Earl of Kenmare (1891- 1943). Viscount Castlerosse until he inherited the Earldom in 1941. Soldier and Journalist. The "Lady Castlerosse" referred to here was Doris Delevingne (1900-1942). Divorced Castlerosse in 1938. He later married Enid, Lady Furness, who survived him.

[289]Cited in The Spectator, 21 December , 1956.

[290] The Sketch Magazine, Volume 86 (1914) has a photograph of Evan with Viscount Castlerosse and a number of other peers and peeresses on board Evan's father yacht Liberty at Cannes.

[291] Leonard Mosley (1913-1992). British writer, historian and journalist.

[292] Moseley, Leonard. ' Castlerosse.' Arthur Barker (1956).

[293] Letters in Tredegar House Archives (from the 1970s) from Evan's friends in particular Henry Maxwell (one of Evan's inner circle) , who reflects on Evan tearing a strip off his butler and others.

[294] Daily Independent Journal (San Rafael). 1 February 1975.

[295] Ibid.

[296] The Ottawa Journal, 24 December, 1936.

[297] Backed by Churchill and Beaverbrook, Edward proposed to broadcast a speech indicating his desire to remain on the throne or to be recalled to it if forced to abdicate, while marrying Simpson morganatically. See Ziegler, Philip. King Edward VIII. Harperpress. (2012).

[298] See Bruce Lockhart, Sir Robert. 'Diaries.' Volume 1. MacMillan. (1973). See also Bruce Lockhart,. Sir Robert. 'Friends, Foes and Foreigners.' Putnam. (1957).

[299] Evan appears in the "PAST OFFICERS" list as "the Hon. E F Morgan" at the 1927 dinner at the Savoy Hotel on Thursday 2 June 1927.

[300] See Sunday Times, 31 May 1931 . Shelia Milbanke (several times married) born Shelia Chisholm, a captivating Australian is the subject of a recent book ' Shelia : The Australian Ingenue who bewitched British Society' by Robert Wainwright, Allen& Unwin. (2014).

[301] Poppy Baring Banking heiress. Helen (known as Poppy) Azalea Baring, Later Mrs William Thursby. (1901-1979).

[302] See Sunday Times, 4 December, 1927 refers to a dance in aid of the rebuilding fund of RADA at Claridges supported by the presence of Prince Edward'. "The Evan was giving supper to Miss Poppy Baring".

[303] The Society drug addict Kiki Preston introduced Prince George to morphine and cocaine and his habit was maintained by Jorge Ferrara, the bisexual son of the Argentine Ambassador. When the Prince of Wales found out, Ferrara was booted out of Britain and George was sent off to countryside, almost certainly with Evan.

[304] There are several accounts of PG's troubles. See Cross, William. 'Not behind Lace Curtains.' Book Midden (2013) and books on Noel Coward by, Philip Hoare and Sheridan Morley. Other names of PG's bed mates include Prince Louis Ferdinand of Prussia and Chips Channon ,He also slept with women, including attractive, bubbly Poppy Baring (whom he wanted to marry, but was forbidden by the King) the ubiquitous Lady (Mary) Bridget Parsons (1907-1972) who was also groomed as a wife candidate for PG (See

Memoirs of Robin Bryans) . He later married the ' fag-hag' Princess Marina of Greece and Denmark.

[305]See Bradford. Sarah. Elizabeth: A Biography of Britain's Queen p46" Prince George threw himself with enthusiasm into London night life....George's closest friends tended to be cultured homosexuals like Prince Paul of Yugoslavia and Chips Channon..."

[306]See Morley. Sheridan. 'Noel Coward.' Aus Publishing. (2005).

[307]See Cross, William.' Not Behind Lace Curtains.' Book Midden Publishing. (2013).

[308]Ibid.

[309] The Court Circular for 22 April, 1935 records " Prince Paul of Greece and Denmark and Viscount Tredegar have returned from the West Indies to Tredegar Park where his Royal Highness will remain for a short stay."

[310] British Library Manuscripts. Add MS 82766. A letter dated 27 October 1935 from Evelyn, Duchess of Devonshire (1870-1960) to Mabell, Countess of Arlie (1866-1956) - both members of Queen Mary's household.

[311]Bryans. Robin. 'Checkmate: Memoirs of a Political Prisoner.' Honeyford Press (1994).

[312] Bruce Lockhart, Sir Robert. 'Sir Robert Bruce Lockhart Diaries 1915-1938.' Macmillan (1973).

[313] See Aldrich. Robert. ' The Seduction of the Mediterranean: Writing, Art and Homosexual Fantasy.' Routledge. (2002).

[314] Bryans. Robin. Checkmate: Memoirs of a Political Prisoner.' Honeyford Press (1994).

[315]Ibid.

[316]Pryce-Jones. Alan. 'The Bonus of Laughter.' Hamish Hamilton (1987).

[317]Ibid.

[318]See Bryans, Robin. 'The Dust Has Never Settled.' Honeyford Press. (1992).

[319] Jessica Doris Delevingne (1900-1942) Divorced by Castlerosse in 1938. She later took her own life, one source Daily Mail (29 July , 2013)) saying" . She retired to her hotel room, took a drink, and with it a fatal overdose of pills."

[320] Moseley, Leonard. 'Castlerosse.' Arthur Barker (1956).

[321]William Randolph Hearst (1863-1951). Americannewspaper publisher. Bought St Donat's in 1925.

[322]Now Atlantic College, an international (residential) 6th Form College and educational centre.

[323]Sir Philip Sassoon (1888-1939) 3rd Baronet. Unmarried, politician and art collector. Sassoon created with others some of the finest country houses at Port Lympne Mansion, Kent and Trent Park, Hertfordshire.

[324]Lowndes Marie Belloc and Lowndes. 'Diaries and Letters of Marie Balloc Lowndes, (1911-1947).' Catto & Windus (1971).

[325] Lee- Milne, James. ' The enigmatic Edwardian: the life of Reginald, 2nd Viscount Esher.' Sidwick & Jackson.(1900).

[326]The Argus (Melbourne) 2 June 1928.

[327]Sassoon is swept into the "homosexual bloc" of his " friend" TE Lawrence and John Maynard Keynes by M Kienholz in " Opium Traders and Their Worlds-Volume Two" iUniverse (2008). However Peter Stansky Sassoon's biographer declares in ' Sassoon: the Worlds of Philip and Sybil' that " No evidence has survived of Philip's sexual activities, although his style would certainly support the idea he was a homosexual, and many assumed hew was."

[328]Philip Tilden (1887-1956). English architect and designer and homosexual.

[329] "Lush and Luxurious" is the title of a short study of Tilden's life and work by James Bettley. RIBA (1987). Bettley cites work done by Tilden for Evan at 40 South Street, Mayfair.

[330]Napier Sturt, 3rd Baron Alington (1896-1940). Married Lady Mary Ashley Cooper, (she died in 1936) one daughter Hon. Mary Anna Sibell Elizabeth Sturt (Mrs Marten) who died in 2010.

[331]Tallulah Bankhead (1902-1968). American actress and diva.

[332]Dickinson, Peter. ' Lord Berners: Composer, Writer, Painter.' Boydell & Brewer Ltd. (2008). Some versions of this anecdote substitute Naps' mother as his companion.

[333] Karol Szymanosski (1882-1937). Polish composer. In 1922 he dedicated his highly sensuous 'Songs of an infatuated Muezzin Op.42' to Naps Alington.

[334]Among Doris' conquests were a cluster of homosexual or bisexual men including Cecil Beaton, Laddie Sanford, Randolph Churchill, Tom Mitford, Robert Herber Percy and William Edward Rootes, of Rootes cars fame. The latter pair was cited by Castlerosse in his divorce petition of 1936. See National Archives, Kew, File J 77/3615/2070. A previous petition named the art collector Sir Alfred Lane Beit as one of Doris' lovers. See National Archives, Kew file J 77/3073/4678. One much quoted remark attributed to Winston Churchill (evidently another of Doris' successes) is that when the old war horse heard that his son Randolph had been involved with Doris he retorted "Doris, you could make a corpse come."

[335] See Daily Mail 19 July, 2013 for an article by Chris Montague on Doris Castlerosse. Lois had flings with Royal Princes, a long affair with Reggie Herbert, 15th Earl of Pembroke and latterly lived with the two men cited by Evan in the cross petition in answer to Lois's proceedings. The action by Lois did not reach the final stages of divorce and lay in abeyance.

[336]See Cross, William and Dart Monty. 'Aspects of Evan.' Book Midden Publishing (2012).

[337] See National Archives. Kew, file J 77/3117/5878.

[338]The horses included race horses, Lois had her own racing colours. As well as a pet Pomeranian dog that lived some of the time at Crichel (the Sturt/Alington seat, in Dorset) she also bred great Danes. Lois lived at Mumpumps, Surrey with stockbroker Captain Alex (Tim) Freeland (1890-1939) and a zoologist named Ernest Boulenger(1888-1946). Boulenger was director of the aquarium at the London Zoo and a popular writer on natural history subjects. Lois met Boulenger many years before when her father (who died in 1919) was still alive.

[339]Daily Mail, 20 December, 1937.

[340] Ibid.

[341] Lois willed that Edward Boulenger have use of her last home and left the residue of the estate to him for life. With the remainder going to her 8-yar-old niece (her brother Naps' daughter) Hon. Mary Sturt. She left £500 to Captain Freeland and one year's wages and her car to chauffeur Leslie Youldon (sometimes recorded as Kingswell).

[342] Hull Daily Mail, 18 December, 1937.

[343] Hon. David Carnegie (1871-1900). Son of the 9th Earl and Countess of Southesk. A memorial to David can be seen in Brechin Cathedral.

[344] The Scotsman, 27 November, 1900. David was working as a local administrator/ soldier in West Africa for Sir Frederick G Lugard (1858-1945), head of the West African Frontier Force.

[345] H Rider Haggard (1856-1925). Writer of adventure stories including King Solomon's Mines.

[346] The Scotsman newspaper of 2 February, 1898 has a long article about this journey by David Carnegie. The Western Mail of Australia of 27 April, 1897 commented "'a white man might suffer the tortures of death from thirst while a dozen paces from him hidden in the tufts of the spinifex (spiny grass) where a few gallons of water which alone could save life. " This expedition put David Carnegie 'in the front rank amongst Australian explorers'.

[347] Godfrey Charles Morgan (1831- 1913). 2nd Lord Tredegar (1875-1913). Unmarried. Known affectionately as ' Godfrey the Good', he endowed many buildings and land to the people of Newport.

[348]The Bulletin, Volume 55. Issue 217-Volume 56, Issue 224. The Society. (2004).

[349]Ibid.

[350] The second section of the book is based on the following files from National Archives.. Kew. LCO 57/382, IR40/11982, IR 62/2705 ad IR 40/9713.

[351] Evan's tax papers show £77,059.19s.1d remitted leaving £10,000 arrears for 19933/34 to be brought forward. The sum of £10,000 was retained as due pending monies into the Estate from Miss Violet Sydney's Trust. The latter

was lady aged over 70, and in death the sum of £10,000 would be due to the personal estate of the incumbent Lord Tredegar.

[352] Sir William Bernard Blatch (1887-1965). Solicitor to the Board of Inland Revenue, 1939 to 1952. Known as "Bernard".

[353] Theodore Henry Edgcome Edwards (1902-1978). Solicitor.

[354] Messrs Stephenson, Harwood and Tatham, solicitors, of Cheapside, London, EC.

[355] Lien = the legal right of a creditor to sell the collateral property of a debtor who fails to meet the obligations of a loan contract.

[356] The Right Honourable Evan Frederick Viscount Tredegar, deceased. Testator died at Honeywood House, Oakwood Hill, Dorking, Surrey on 27th April 1949. Grant of Probate, save and except Settled Land, issued out of Principal Probate Registry on the 29th December 1949. Executors: The Right Honourable Charles Alexander, Earl of Southesk, K.C.V.O. of Kinnaird Castle, Brechin, Angus Scotland., Major Raymond Alexander Carnegie of Crimonmogate Loumay, Aberdeenshire, Scotland and Theodore Henry Edgcome Edwards Esq of 2 Orchard Gardens, Teignmouth, Devon. Power reserved to the Right Honourable Theobald Walter Somerset, Earl of Carrick. NOTE: The Estate, being insolvent, was administered under the directions of the Board of Inland Revenue.

[357] To reflect tax due the sum of £8,026 was accounted for on the Revenue papers in respect of the full value of Emily Sutherland's annuity.

[358] Sir Robert Waterer, CB. Solicitor of Inland Revenue 1952 to 1956. Died 1971 aged 80.

[359] The Revenue files contain this statement: "See below regarding the matters raised in the final paragraph of the Solicitors report of the 8th December 1954, the memorandum attached hereunder has been furnished by the Special Contribution P.C. on the first point. With regard to the second point relating to the payments and set offs, the position appears to be, from these surtax papers, that, at the present time, there are no sums held on deposit, all payments having been brought to account as will be seen from the tabular statement annexed hereunder. Thus is an extension of page 13 of the Executors Accounts accompanying the Solicitors report on the Taxes papers and shows the disposal of each of the payments and set offs. When the allocation of the various payments was decided, the relative sums on deposit were brought to account and receipts giving particulars of the surtax satisfied thereby were issued by the Accountant General (Cashier). It seems therefore, that Messrs Tozers have already received notification of the allocations. The Estate Duty of some £3,000, mentioned towards the end of the report referred to, no doubt, be satisfied out of the expected further payment of £4,800. The

two set-offs referred to are confirmed and were allocated as shown" 29th December 1954.

360 J H Stamp was one of the great characters at the English bar. He was a Chancery barrister for well over 50 years. He died in 1964, aged 93.

361   TREDEGAR SETTLED LAND ACT CLAIM

SOUTHESK – v – RODNEY

JOINT OPINION

In our opinion the application if now renewed would be unlikely to succeed

Likely.   Mr. Justice Roxburgh did not appear favourably disposed to the application and although he took the course of requiring further evidence rather than dismissing it out of hand it is easy to see in what respect the evidence already before the court could usefully be supplemented. In fact such further evidence as could be made available merely serves to emphasise the extravagant expenditure of the late Lord Tredegar and we think it most unlikely that this further evidence would induce Mr. Justice Roxburgh to accede to the application.

We think that another Judge might well have taken a different view of the application in the first place. But faced by the negative attitude of Mr. Justice Roxburgh on the original hearing and the absence of any further evidence of a helpful character another Judge would, we think, find great difficulty in reaching in effect a different conclusion from that of Mr. Justice Roxburgh.

In our opinion the only hope of success would be to restore the summons at a date when it will be heard by a different Judge; endorsements on our briefs do not indicate that Mr. Justice Roxburgh retained it. But for the reasons given above we should regard this course as speculative and having regard in particular to the heavy burden of preparing further evidence and the 75 per cent recompense in estate duty it may be considered better to let the application drop at this stage

(Sgd) J. Pennycuick   (Sgd) J. H. Stamp.

362 Even before Courtenay's death he was in difficulties over payment of tax and at the time of his death (according to Evan's tax papers) there were considerable arrears of surtax for five years.

[363] Evan's Executors wrote to the Inland Revenue "You will recollect that the Executors continue to hold £250 4½% Founder Debentures of Phyllis Court Members Club Limited. We have been trying for years to find a purchaser without success and now we are informed by the Accountants of the club that a member would be willing to offer £18 - 15 - 0 for these Debentures. The Accountant's letter contains the following paragraph: "The reason for such a low offer is of course that the club has been going through a pretty bad time financially and the interest has been waived by most holders for very many years and, furthermore, that being a members club there is really no prospect of surpluses occurring and therefore these debentures can only have a purely nominal value". So far as the Executors go the interest at 4½% has always been received because they have not felt as trustees they could waive it. The Inland Revenue file records: "These debentures are the only assets remaining of this estate, except possibly a small amount of income apportionments due from the settled estates. The interest has, however been regularly paid since the death of the deceased, and accordingly the offer of £18.15.0. which is less than two years purchase of the gross interest seems rather meagre."

[364] Reference to Miss Violet Sidney or Sydney is unclear. She was a beneficiary under a Tredegar family trust. The sum of £10,000 was due to fall into the personal estate of Evan. The original Trust was set up on 5 February 1901 by Godfrey Morgan, the 2nd Lord Tredegar. Violet Sydney was born on 4 February 1877.

[365] A report dated 6 January 1950 from E Kingsley Read of the Institute of Actuaries estimates the "present value of the Settled Estate, after payment of all outstanding duties and expenses is in the neighbourhood of £1,000,000". This figure was deemed conservative by Inland Revenue. An analysis of Evan's indicated Real Estate £1,500,000, Heirlooms £20,000. Capital Monies £298,403 and Securities (under compensation under the Coal Act) £ 538,682. Total £ 2,357,085.

[366] This proposed purchase is mentioned in July, 1949, by a Mr Weston (colleague of Sir Bernard Blatch). The process was handed by Mr J Smith of Rider Heaton Meredith & Mills on behalf of John through the Executors of Courtenay's Estate which bizarrely included John's father, Frederick George. This was later estimated (independently) to be worth £6000. An adjustment to £8,000 was suggested by Rider, Heaton Meredith & Mills (as the Revenue thought this was on the low side). There was also a concern about John's bachelor status, as this affected the tax position on the interest and the income would still be taxable unless John married and at death left male issue over 21. John did subsequently marry, in 1954 but had no children. The interest reversion was worth (various amounts stated) between £60,000 and £200,000. This issue went through a protracted legal process at which time

the value of the interest rose substantially. On 26 April 1955 John's solicitors offered £20,000 for the purchase of the reversion on Courtenay's Estate, including the interest in Violet Sydney's Trust Fund. After further arguments and meetings a settlement was reached for £20,000. An adjusting payment was made of £ 20,178.19s.3d and the outstanding tax arrears from Courtenay's Estate were reduced accordingly, with £66,880.19s.10d being given up.

Tozers also sent a cheque to the Revenue for £5,000 which was incorrectly allocated to what was outstanding on Courtenay's tax arrears. This was latter amended to reduce Evan's tax debts.

[367] Inland Revenue Assessments Division file records: "This was a case in which the Board's Solicitor supervised the Revenue claim, consisting mainly of very large Surtax arrears in the deceased's insolvent estate. The Assessment Division was called in to advise on questions of allocation of payments and Post War Credit. We never took over arrears or managed the Revenue claim. Our activity was completed in early 1956 but the papers were held by the Solicitor of Inland Revenue for some time. On 1/8/56 Mr. Price sent a memo to Assessment Division to which Mr. Every replied on 20/8/56: "Papers seen and returned with thanks. A 600/45038 have been P.A." Our papers were then put away accordingly."

APPENDIX 1

Evan Frederic Morgan, Viscount Tredegar
Executor's Final Statement

<u>The Right Honourable Evan Frederic Viscount Tredegar, deceased</u>

<u>Testator died</u> at Honeywood House, Oakwood Hill, Dorking Surrey on the 27th April 1949

<u>Grant of Probate, save and except Settled Land, issued</u> out of the Principal Probate Registry on the 29th December 1949

<u>Executors:-</u>

The Right Honourable Charles Alexander Earl of Southesk, K.C.V.O of Kinnaird Castle, Brechin, Angus, Scotland.

Mayor Raymond Alexander Carnegie of CrimonmogateLonmay Aberdeen, Scotland and

Theodore Henry Edgcome Edwards Esq of 2 Orchard Gardens, Teignmouth, Devon.

Power reserved to the Right Honourable Theobald Walter Somerset, Earl of Carrick

NOTE

The Estate, being insolvent, was administered under the directions of the Board of Inland Revenue.

The Right Honourable Charles Alexander Earl of Southesk, K.C.V.O
Major Raymond Alexander Carnegie and Theodore Henry Edgecome
Edwards Esq

NB The amounts are in pounds, shillings and pence

SCHEDULE OF DEBTS PAID BY EXECUTORS BY DIRECTION OF BOARD OF INLAND REVENUE				
By Cash paid Art & Book Shop	Booksellers	86	17	-
Antique Art Galleries Ltd.,	Antiques	51	19	-
Atlantis Bookshop	Booksellers	15	17	6
Arcade Gallery Ltd.,	Antiques	9	-	-
Asprey& Co Ltd.,	Watch repairers	211	7	-
Charles Agate	Agricultural Merchant	14	2	11
Burns Oates &Washbourne Ltd	Book dealers	4	11	10
Bernard Quarich Ltd	Book dealers	58	17	6
Bell John &Croyden	Chemists		7	-
George Biddle & Son Ltd	Art dealers	67	-	-
Bluett& Sons	Antique dealers	62	10	-

Berkeley Galleries Ltd	Antique dealers	184	-	-
Alan G Berry Esq	Veterinary	1	1	-
Norman Brett Ltd	Bookmakers	7	6	8
Miss Eileen Conway	Wages	22	19	8
Cartier Limited	Jewellers	393	10	-
Central House Hotel	Board & residence	11	-	-
Dr Gerald de Lacey	Professional services	96	-	-
Dunkin & Co Ltd	Stationers		17	1
Dixeys Ltd	Opticians		2	6
Lewis Davis & Son	Jewellers	132	10	-
Daimler Co. Ltd, re accident	Balance paid by insurance	5	16	8
Daimler Hire Co. Ltd.	Ambulance hire	9	-	-
Mrs Nora Dickson	Hotel account	1	18	-
A J Edser	Grocer	8	3	7
Evershed & Cripps Ltd	Grocers	15	1	9
L Franklin	Jeweller	10	10	-
Fortnum & Mason	Grocers	10	13	10
J Kyrle Fletcher	Antique dealers	19	8	6
IfanKyrle Fletcher	Rare books	3	11	-
Grays	Chemists	2	9	6
Thomas Goode & Co	China & Glass dealers	7	13	6
Dr Gwen Hilton	Professional services	52	10	-
H.R. Hancock & Sons	Antique dealers	6	-	-

Hatchards Ltd	Booksellers	1	6	3
A Hull & Sons	Fruiterer & Florists	7	13	0
Harrods Ltd	Grocers	1	1	15
Harrods Ltd	Estate Agent &Valuers	57	0	6
Robert Jackson & Co. Ltd	Grocers	7	5	6
-ditto-	Provisions	9	17	-
Jackson Brothers	Automobile Engineers	189	17	8
E T Lane & Sons Ltd	Art Furnishers	10	17	8
H. & E. Lincott Ltd	Engineers	7	18	-
Luzac& Co. Ltd	Booksellers	35	14	6
Sydney L. Moss	Antique Dealer	110	-	-
Meyer Mortimer Ltd	Tailors	73	3	-
Morgan & Ball	Tailors	33	5	-
Jack Naughton	Wages	7	3	3
H. R. N Norton	Antique Dealer	137	10	-
Peat, Warwick, Mitchell & Co.,	Professional Services	895	-	-
Pugh &McCormac	Veterinary Surgeons	12	18	6
Postmaster General	Telephone accounts at Honeywood House	82	18	3
Pleasance & Harper Ltd.,	Jewellers	2	3	-
Routledge&Kegan Paul Ltd.,	Booksellers	7	10	11

Regina Bureau Ltd.,	Servants Agency		7	2
Roberts & Co.,	Chemists		5	6
Dorking &Herley Rural District Council	Proportion of rates on Honeywood House & Lodge from 1 April to 3rd May 1949	5	12	4
	Forward	£3281	18	5

SCHEDULE OF DEBTS (Contd)	Forward £	3281	18	5
BY Horsham Rural District Council	Rates on Honeybush Cottage & Rose Cottage Rowhook from 1st April to 3rd May 1949	12	3	9
Regency Antique Gallery Ltd	Antique Dealers	24	15	-

J. Stanton Reddich	Balance owing on picture sold by Deceased	23	-	-
Dr S. Cochrane Sharks	X-Ray services	4	4	-
Spink& Son Ltd	Antique Dealers	424	5	6
John Sparks Ltd	" "	359	10	-
Charles J. Sawyer Ltd	Book Sellers	60	8	4
Sodastream Ltd	Soda Water Machine Manufacturers	1	12	8
W. G. Scott-Brown	Professional attendance	5	5	-
C. E. A. Smith	Car Hire	59	3	3
South Eastern Electricity Board		58	1	-
J. H. Sayers	Fishmonger		18	2
J.P.L. Sumner	Hay Merchant	33	-	-
Dr Cedric Shaw	Professional services	26	5	
W. H. Smith & Son Ltd	Newsagents	1	14	8
Toogood& Sons Ltd	Seed growers	8	5	4

Times Book Club	Booksellers	2	16	6
Tyler & Co Ltd	Wines & Spirits	21	4	-
P. G. Tyler	Loan to deceased	16	-	-
University College Hospital	Maintenance	38	1	2
A Worsfold& Son	Coal Merchants	16	5	6
Messrs Duckett	Good supplied	2	13	6
Sir Russel Wilkinson	Professional attendances	66	12	-
Stephen Coyne	Good supplied	2	10	11
W.O Connor & Sons, Dublin	Tailors	11	11	-
Messrs RobtDrane Ltd	Chemists		9	3
Devonshire Hand Laundry		2	18	9

"Debts due to creditors resident abroad:-

Mr Louis Decostier		20	-	-
Dr. Giovanni Mazzetta		29	7	-
Dr Sandoz		81	15	4
Dr A.M.Jeans		11	6	8

		£	4708	1	8

APPENDIX 2

LAST WILL AND TESTAMENT OF EVAN MORGAN
Pages Follow 198-201

N72

In His Majesty's High Court of Justice.

The Principal Probate Registry.

BE IT KNOWN that The Right Honourable EVAN FREDERIC (in the will spelt Frederick) VISCOUNT TREDEGAR of Tredegar Park Newport Monmouthshire and Honeywood House Oakwood Hill Dorking Sussex

died at Honeywood House aforesaid on the 27th day of April 19_

having made and duly executed his last Will and Testament

That on the 29th day of December 19_ Probate of the said Will Principal save and except Settled Land was granted at the Probate Registry to The Right Honourable Charles Alexander Earl of Southesk K.C.V.O. The Honourable Raymond Alexander Carnegie and Theodore Henry Edgcome Edwards three of the executors named in the said will power being reserved to the other executors

AND BE IT FURTHER KNOWN that at the date hereunder written the last Will and Testament (a copy whereof is hereunto annexed)

of the said deceased was proved in the Principal Probate Registry of His Majesty's High Court of Justice and that Administration of the Estate of the said deceased was granted by the aforesaid Court to The Honourable CHARLES CHRISTIAN SIMON RODNEY of 43 Bishopsgate London E.C.2 Major (retired) Grenadier Guards one of the Trustees at the date of death of the said deceased of settled land vested in the said deceased under one indenture of Settlement dated the 1st day of July 1896 and as such land The Right Honourable Theobald Walter Somerset Henry Earl of Carrick and Sir Robert John Walter Knight two others of the trustees at the date of death of the said deceased and no such two other of the executors no to the said settled land having heretofore renounced probate limited to the said settled land and The Right Honourable Frederic George Lord Tredegar the other trustee at the date of death of the said deceased and no such the other executor as to the said settled land having retired from the Trust ... By order on Summons ...

And it is hereby certified that an Affidavit for Inland Revenue has been delivered wherein it is shewn that the gross value of the said Estate in England amounts to £1520000 — 0 — 0

And it is further certified that it appears ...

Dated the 19th day of January 1951

Registrar.

Extracted by Rider Heaton Meredith & Mills
8 New Square Lincoln's Inn London W.C.2

IN THE NAME OF THE HOLY AND UNDIVIDED TRINITY AMEN

I THE RIGHT HONOURABLE EVAN FREDERICK VISCOUNT TREDEGAR Second Viscount
of the Second Creation of Tredegar Park Newport in the County of Monmouth and
of Honeywood House Oakwood Hill Dorking in the County of Surrey and an Oblate
of St. Mary's Abbey Buckfast in the County of Devon DECLARE this to be my
last Will and Testament

1.   I REVOKE all Wills and testamentary dispositions heretofore made by me

2.   I APPOINT the Right Honourable Charles Alexander Earl of Southesk K.C.V.O.
the Right Honourable Theobald Walter Somerset Earl of Carrick the Honourable
Raymond Alexander Carnegie and Theodore Henry Edgcome Edwards of Teignmouth in
the County of Devon Solicitor (hereinafter together called "my Executors") to
be the Executors and Trustees of this my Will

3.   I DESIRE to be buried in the private cemetery of Buckfast Abbey AND I
DECLARE that by the provisions of this my Will I wish to leave a testimony of
my sincere attachment to the Abbot and Monks serving God and Our Lady St.
Mary in the restored Abbey of Buckfast

4.   I GIVE the following legacies free of duty namely:-

(a) To Mrs. Emily Sutherland (my late Secretary) my jewel box with all the
contents thereof at the date of my death (excepting the ring said to have been
used by the Black Prince and the rings bearing my crest initial and coronet)

(b) To my Valet provided he shall have been in my service for three years
prior to my death and not under notice whether given or received all my
wearing apparel (save my rings robes coronet medals chains and other insignia
of rank or office) but if no such person exists I give the same to the Head
House in England of the Order of St. Vincent de Paul with the request that
they will sell the same and distribute the proceeds for the benefit of such
sick or poor persons as they may in their absolute discretion select

(c) To such of my friends Henry Maxwell (son of W.B. Maxwell) and Cyril
Hartman B.Litt of University College Oxford as shall be living at my death and
if more than one equally between them all my books concerning myself or
written by myself at present in the sitting room at Honeywood House aforesaid
and all documents of a personal nature whether comprising manuscripts in my
own hand or typescript together with all my personal letters and papers
contained in several tins and other boxes and without imposing any binding on

M6

legal obligation on them I express my desire that they will from the information
to be obtained from such books papers and documents be able to write a
biography of my life _____

(d) To the Louvre Museum at Paris my erotic bronze statuette of Satyr by
A. Rodin _____

(e) To the Trustees for the time being of a Deed of Settlement dated the First
day of July One thousand eight hundred and ninety-six as amended or varied by a
Deed dated the Sixteenth day of June One thousand nine hundred and nine under
which I am at present a tenant for life in possession of the Tredegar Settled
Estates and of certain heirlooms UPON TRUST that such trustees shall hold the
same upon the trusts and subject to the powers terms and provisions contained
in the said Deeds as if such items had been included therein as heirlooms to
the extent that such items shall as from the date of my death devolve and be
enjoyed as heirlooms with the Tredegar Settled Estates and heirlooms the
following articles namely:-

> The picture of Tredegar Park executed by Algernon Newton R.A. in 1940
> All tapestries or needlework pictures _____
> My portrait in oils by Cathleen Mann (Marchioness of Queensberry)
> The portrait of myself painted in 1928 by William Rankin A.A.
> The portrait of my mother in a green coat by Sir Augustus John O.M.
> My swords medals robes coronet chains and other insignia of office
> My rings bearing my crest initial and coronet _____
> My Queen Mary four-poster bed _____

(f) To the Trustees for the time being of St. Mary's Abbey Buckfast all the
remainder of my personal chattels as defined by Section 55 (1) (x) of the
Administration of Estates Act 1925 upon trust for the general charitable
purposes of the Community of Benedictine Monks residing at the said Abbey

5.   I DECLARE that the decision of my Executors as to what articles pass
under any of the gifts hereinbefore specified shall be final and binding on
all persons concerned _____

6.   I GIVE all my property not hereby or by any Codicil hereto otherwise
specifically disposed of and including all property which I can dispose of by
Will in any manner I think proper either as beneficially entitled thereto or
under any general power unto my Executors UPON TRUST to sell call in and
convert the same into money with power to postpone such sale calling in and

2

146.

conversion so long as my Executors in their absolute discretion think fit and after payment out of the money arising thereby or out of my ready money of my debts funeral and testamentary expenses and the duty on all legacies given free of duty TO HOLD the residue of such monies upon trust to transfer the same to the Trustees for the time being of St. Mary's Abbey Buckfast aforesaid for the general charitable purposes of the Community of Benedictine Monks residing at the said Abbey AND I DESIRE that the Trustees of the said Abbey shall arrange for one Mass to be said each week for the period of seven years from the date of my death for the Repose of my Soul

7.

ANY Executor or Trustee hereof being a Solicitor or other person engaged in any profession or business may be so employed or act and shall be entitled to charge and be paid all professional or other charges for any business or act done by him or his firm in connection with the administration of my estate and the trusts hereof including acts which an executor or trustee not being a Solicitor or other person engaged as aforesaid could have done personally

IN WITNESS whereof I have to this my Will set my hand this 3th day of March in the year of the Incarnation of Our Lord and Saviour Jesus Christ One thousand nine hundred and forty eight

SIGNED by the Testator the said
RIGHT REVERENT REV. PATRICK
MONSIGN MONSIGN as and for his
last Will and Testament in the
presence of us both being present
at the same time who at his request
in his presence and in the presence
of each other have hereunto subscribed
our names as witnesses

Thanks and Acknowledgements

The Author wishes to thank *everyone* who has been involved in the preparation of this book. Particular thanks must go to the late Robin Bryans, Bernard Byrom, Monty and Tom Dart, Bernard Pearson, The British Library, National Library of Wales, The National Trust, Tredegar Archives, National Archives, Kew, and Newport Reference Library staff.

Author Declaration

The Author graciously acknowledges the various Authors of material quoted in the text and End Notes and their respective publishers and copyright holders. Such quotes used have been kept modest and incidental. Care has been taken *not* to exceed the spirit of the copyright principles laid down in the respective *"Permissions and Fair Dealing"* guidelines in terms of the limits under the criteria for *"the purposes of criticism or review"*.

About William Cross

William Cross (Will) spent 28 years as a Civil Servant, in London. He took early retirement in July 2005 to concentrate on writing and research. His roots are Scottish; his family origins are in Erskine, Renfrewshire and Kilmaronock, Loch Lomondside. Will was brought up in a small coal-mining village in Lanarkshire. After schooldays in Scotland he studied at the Universities of London and Southampton. He now lives in Wales. Will is the author (or co-author) of three books on the Morgans of Tredegar House, Newport, South Wales and five books on the Carnarvons (Herberts) of Highclere Castle, Hampshire. He is currently working on a new book for issue in 2015, including ' Rosemary and Alastair' : "Everything is More Beautiful Because We're Doomed" about the ill-fated daughter and son of Millie, Duchess of Sutherland.

Will is a Fellow of the Society of Antiquaries of Scotland, he regularly lectures on Scottish history topics, the Morgan

Women of Tredegar House and on the Carnarvons. Will is also a Member of the Society of Authors. He is married with two grown up sons and two grandchildren. Contact Will by email: williecross@aol.com

Visit Will's Web Site http://will-cross-author.yolasite.com/

Other Titles from Book Midden Publishing
These titles are written by William Cross

The Abergavenny Witch Hunt : An account of the prosecution of over twenty homosexuals in a small Welsh town in 1942. ISBN 9781905914227

Not Behind Lace Curtains: The Hidden World of Evan, Viscount Tredegar. ISBN 9781985914210

The Life and Secrets of Almina Carnarvon: A Candid Biography of Almina, 5th Countess of Carnarvon. 3rd Edition. ISBN 9781905914081

Lordy! Tutankhamun's Patron As A Young Man. ISBN 9781905914050

These are by Monty Dart & William Cross

A Beautiful Nuisance by Monty Dart and William Cross. ISBN 9781905914104

Aspects of Evan by Monty Dart and William Cross ISBN 9781905914159

Other Titles

Daphne's Story: The Long Journey from the Red Brick Building by Daphne Condon. ISBN 9781905914128

Steaming Light: by Bernard Pearson. ISBN 9781905914135

Who Killed Dripping Lewis? By Monty Dart ISBN 9781905914199

Forthcoming Titles from Book Midden Publishing

More Secrets About Almina, Fifth Countess of Carnarvon: The Pocket Venus of Highclere Castle. By William Cross. ISBN 9782905914296

Rosemary and Alastair: "Everything is More Beautiful Because We're Doomed": By William Cross. ISBN 9781905914289

The Five Lady Tredegars: Of Tredegar House, Newport, South Wales. By Monty Dart and William Cross. ISBN 9781905914203

Contact Book Midden by e-mail <u>williecross@aol.com</u>

Evan Frederic Morgan, the last Viscount Tredegar